Physical Characteristics
Cairn Terrier
(from the American Kennel Club breed standard)

Body: Well-muscled, strong, active body with well-sprung, deep ribs, coupled to strong hindquarters, with a level back of medium length, giving an impression of strength and activity without heaviness.

Tail: In proportion to head, well furnished with hair but not feathery. Carried gaily but must not curl over back. Set on at back level.

Coat: Hard and weather-resistant. Must be double-coated with profuse harsh outer coat and short, soft, close furry undercoat.

Color: May be of any color except white. Dark ears, muzzle and tail tip are desirable.

Ideal Size: Weight for bitches, 13 pounds; for dogs, 14 pounds. Height at the withers: bitches, 9.5 inches; dogs, 10 inches. Length of body from 14.25 to 15 inches from the front of the chest to back of hindquarters.

Cairn Terrier

◇

By Robert Jamieson

Contents

KENNEL CLUB BOOKS: CAIRN TERRIER
ISBN: 1-59378-235-7

Copyright © 1999 • **Revised American Edition: Copyright © 2004**
Kennel Club Books, Inc., 308 Main Street, Allenhurst, NJ 07711 USA
Cover Design Patented: US 6,435,559 B2 • Printed in South Korea

Photos by Alice van Kempen with additional photographs by :
Norvia Behling, T. J. Calhoun, Carolina Biological Supply, Doskocil,
Isabelle Français, James Hayden-Yoav, James R. Hayden, RBP,
Bill Jonas, Dwight R. Kuhn, Dr. Dennis Kunkel,
Mikki Pet Products, Phototake, Jean Claude Revy,
Dr. Andrew Spielman and C. James Webb.

Illustrations by Renée Low

Even though the
Cairn Terrier is
an ancient breed,
it was officially
recognized by
the English
Kennel Club in
the early 1900s.

HISTORY OF THE
CAIRN TERRIER

The Cairn Terrier is the plucky little dog that hails from the rugged Scottish Highlands. Although this is a game dog with an all-terrier disposition, he is also a loving companion whether he lives in an apartment in the city or in a large house in the country.

This book will give you the history, description and the standard of the Cairn Terrier. You will also learn about puppy care, training and the health of the breed. With the color photographs, you will see that this terrier is cute as a button and a wonderful companion.

This may not be the dog for everyone as terriers are active, busy dogs and this breed is no exception. However, if you like a lively dog, one who will be a devoted family member, this may be the dog for you. And, as is true with most other breeds, once you give your heart and home to a Cairn Terrier, you will remain a devotee to the breed for a lifetime.

HISTORY OF THE BREED
In the history of the dog world, the Cairn Terrier is a fairly ancient breed. However, its official beginnings with The Kennel Club of England, dating back to the early 1900s, places it as one of the more recently recognized terrier breeds. The Cairn Terrier belongs to the group of dogs described as terriers, from the Latin word *terra*, meaning earth. The terrier is a dog that has been bred to work beneath the ground

The Cairn's instinctive keenness is well displayed by Dhoran, seen here with Miss Margaret Warner, granddaughter of Lord Borwick who was so influential in the development of the Cairn Terrier.

to drive out small and large rodents and other animals that can be a nuisance to country living.

All of the dogs in the Terrier Group originated in the British Isles with the exception of the Miniature Schnauzer, whose origins, of course, trace to Germany. Many of the terrier breeds were derived from a similar ancestor. As recently as the mid-1800s, the terriers fell roughly into two basic categories: the rough-coated, short-legged dogs of Scotland and the longer legged, smooth-coated dogs of England.

The family of Scotch Terriers—those bred in Scotland—divide themselves into the modern Scottish Terrier, the West Highland White Terrier, the Cairn Terrier and the Skye Terrier. In the early 1800s, dogs referred to as Scotch Terriers

> ### WHAT'S IN A NAME
> What is a cairn? Webster's Dictionary defines cairn as a "heap of stone piled up as a memorial or as a landmark." Piles of stones in the Highlands marked the graves of the ancient Roman soldiers. In time, brambles, bushes and brush overgrew the rocks and the cairns became ideal places where vermin could make their homes, unseen by man. This was the terrain where the little dog, which was eventually called the Cairn Terrier, plied his skill and earned his name.

could be any one of these breeds. Interbreeding was common among these breeds, and it was not unusual during the 1800s that all of these breeds could come from one litter with color being the deciding factor as to how a particular pup should be classified. J. W. Benyon wrote in his book *The Cairn Terrier*, "The Cairn, the West Highland White and the Scottish Terrier were so similar in the early days that the three were inbred with impunity. Early pedigrees of these breeds would show all three breeds in the lineage of a single dog and the three breeds often came from the same litter, sold according to what the buyer wanted." As breeders started exhibiting at dog shows, it was realized that there must be more uniformity within

The West Highland White Terrier arguably derived from the Cairn Terrier, originally varying only in color.

the breed, i.e., all pups in a litter should look alike as well as being of the same type as their sire and dam.

Much of the early history of the Cairn centers on the Isle of Skye. Take a look at your map of the British Isles and note the remoteness of Skye. It is located to the west of the Highlands and it is part of the Inner Hebrides, a land noted for its rugged typography and tough Scotsmen, where a fearless and tough dog was required to keep the vermin under control. The Cairn, with his large heart and a larger amount of courage, fit the bill for cleaning out vermin in the houses and stables and for clearing the fields and surrounding areas of badgers and foxes. The Cairn history may be a bit convoluted, as the history of many canine breeds is, but it is thought that the oldest strain came from Captain Mac Leod of Drynock on the Isle of Skye.

In the early years the Cairn was called the Short-haired Skye Terrier and on the mainland he was often called the Tod-hunter. In addition to the Mac Leods, who preferred the dogs of silver-gray color, other strains of the Cairn were bred by the Mac Donalds of Watermist, who bred dogs of gray and brindle color, and the Mac Kinnons of Kilbride, who bred the cream, red and dark brindle dogs. All three of these strains form the basis for our present-day Cairn.

The other breed on the Isle of Skye was the Skye Terrier, the long-backed, heavy-bodied dog with the flowing coat. The Skye

The Cairn was probably developed on the Isle of Skye, as was another Scotch Terrier, the Skye Terrier. The Skye is distinctive for his large geometric head and long caterpillar-like body.

The Scottish Terrier, one of the four modern-day breeds that derived from the Scotch Terrier family, is a blood relative of the Cairn.

One of England's most popular ladies in the 1920s was Miss Joyce Pilkington. She owned a red Cairn known as Mickie that went wherever Miss Pilkington went.

Terrier breeders did not like it that the newcomer should be called the Short-haired Skye Terrier! An early pioneer and ardent supporter of the breed was Mrs. Alastair Campbell, founder of the Brocaire Kennels, who had made frequent trips to the Isle of Skye where she purchased her original dogs. She was the first to enter the breed in a dog show. In 1907, she registered Calla Mhor and Cuillean Bhan as Prick-eared Skye Terriers and entered them in a dog show. Later she registered Rog Mhor, who became the sire of one of the first winners of Challenge Certificates (CC), the "tickets" required to gain a championship in the UK. By

1910, The Kennel Club moved the breed to the classification at dog shows of "Any other breed or variety" and 24 dogs were registered. The breed was rapidly gaining in popularity even though it still did not have an official name and there was still confusion about which class the dogs should be entered in at dog shows.

In the meantime, the Skye Terrier fancy was still disturbed by the name "Short-haired Skye Terriers" and protested to The Kennel Club. It was suggested that the breed be called the "Cairn Terrier of Skye," which eventually was shortened to Cairn Terrier. Through the efforts of Mrs. Campbell, who worked prodigiously on the background of the breed and its breeders, The Kennel Club transferred all Short-haired Skyes to the new registry of Cairn Terriers. In the meantime, in October 1911, an official standard was drawn up for the Cairn at the Scottish

THE COURAGEOUS CAIRN
The late Dr. Dieter Fleig in his book *History of Fighting Dogs* wrote, "Specialists for rat killing in England naturally were dogs with terrier blood in their veins. For this purpose you needed not only a brave dog, which did not shy away from rat bites, but one of truly great speed."

Kennel Club show in Edinburgh as breeders realized that there must be uniformity within the breed. By May 29, 1912, the Cairn Terrier had finally obtained his official status with The Kennel Club and Challenge Certificates were now offered at specific shows.

In addition to the backing of Mrs. Campbell, the breed received early support from Lord Hawke and his sisters Mary and Betty, who had imported terriers from Skye from the Watermist strain. Their dogs, Bridget, Bride and Bruin were "road markers" in the breed's early history. The first Cairn champion was Gesto, owned by Mrs. Campbell.

When World War I started, dog breeding and showing in England basically came to a halt. However, as soon as the war was over, the Cairn's popularity immediately began to rise. New

> ### THE INTERESTING CAIRN
> Robert Leighton judged the Skye Terriers at Crufts in 1909. He discovered additional classes under the name of "Short-haired Skyes." He later wrote, "Properly speaking, they were not Skye Terriers...but they were certainly interesting. Small, active, game and very hard in appearance, they were strongly though slimly built...and the more I handled them the more I admired them."

exhibitors joined Mrs. Campbell, and by 1923 over 1,000 Cairns were registered.

Harviestoun Raider, whelped in 1919 and owned by J. E. Kerr, became the first great sire of the breed, producing 11 champions, which was a record for the time. Raider stamped his progeny with his wonderful substance, which was sometimes too much for the judges, and passed along all of his best attributes. At the time, Raider was in the background of two-thirds of all Cairn pedigrees.

By the mid-1920s, Mrs. N. Fleming of Out of the West Kennels was an active breeder and remained so well into the 1930s. Her Fisherman Out of the West and his sire, Doughall Out of the West, were also two

Many members of the Royal Family were dog lovers and possessed several excellent examples of pure-bred dogs. Jaggers was among the two Cairns. The sketch is by Ernest H. Mills.

In the mid-1930s, Her Royal Highness the Princess Royal had a favorite Cairn named Peggy, which was frequently seen in her company.

kennels were disbanded when breeders found that there was not enough food to keep a kennel running. Some hardy souls did manage to keep a few dogs and, when the war ended, breeding and dog showing resumed as it had after World War I.

In 1943 Splinter produced a son by the name of Sport of Zellah. With approval of The Kennel Club, the new owner changed his name to Bonfire of Twobees and he was bred in 1948 to Redletter My Choice, owned by Walter Bradshaw. Attention must be given to the Redletter Kennels of Mr. Bradshaw because of the huge influence, throughout Great Britain and North America that the kennel had on the Cairn Terrier. Through the decades, the kennel established a phenomenal record of show wins and top producers.

important sires throughout the 1920s. In 1933 the great Ch. Splinter of Twobees was whelped. The winner of eight Challenge Certificates, he made his mark not in the show ring but with his influence as a sire with his ability to stamp his type and quality onto his get and their next generations. Over 100 champions in England can trace their pedigrees back to him. In addition, he is in the background of many American champions.

Again, with the advent of World War II, dog breeding came to a halt in Great Britain. Many

THE MORE THINGS CHANGE

The Cairn Terrier, as depicted in paintings from the late 1800s, looks very much like the present-day Cairn. From Mrs. Campbell's Calla Mhor to Ch. Splinter of Twobees to Ch. Cairnwoods Quince, the Cairn Terrier has remained the same in size, structure and coat. This is somewhat unusual, as in many breeds the dog may become significantly larger, or smaller, and there will often be major changes in coat and trimming styles.

Mr. Bradshaw started in dogs in the 1920s, raising Flat-coated Retrievers. Shortly before World War II, he became interested in the Cairn Terrier. The breeding of Redletter My Choice to Bonfire Twobees produced Redletter Mc Joe, who became a champion before the age of two years. He was campaigned in the ring for three years and produced nine champions. His son Ch. Redletter Mc Murran won 26 Challenge Certificates and was the first Cairn to win an all-breed Best in Show at a Championship Show (1956). His daughter, Ch. Redletter Elford Mhorag won 18 CCs. Mc Murran and Mhorag, half-siblings, won both the dog

This historical photo from the 1920s was captioned as follows: "The selling of puppies in the street is a sight of London. Here every pocket may contain a puppy or something of doggie interest. The salesmen are often fanciers and are allowed to 'tell the tale'."

and bitch CCs at five Championship Shows. Ch. Redletter Mc Bryan won 17 CCs and sired 13 champions. Ch. Redletter Twinlaw Seaspirit, who was the second Cairn to win a Best in Show at a Championship Show, was later purchased by Betty Hyslop of Cairndainia Kennels in Canada. Ch. Redletter Marcel won 16 CCs in a single year. Mr. Bradshaw died in 1982 at the age of 86, having made up 42 English champions and having had a major impact on the Cairn Terrier world that may not be repeated any time soon.

Other kennels that have made considerable contributions to the Cairn have been: Mrs. E. H. Drummond's Blencathra Kennels, producer of 25 English

Kim, the favorite Cairn of Miss Violet Petrie, daughter of Blanche, Lady Petrie (a famed aristocrat of the 1920s), is here seen with her owner.

champions; the Toptwig Kennels of Mrs. Gladys Marsh, which exported dogs to the United States and Sweden, making an impact in both countries; Mrs. H. L. Manley of Lofthouse Kennels, producing 10 English champions and exporting winning dogs to the US; Oudenarde Kennels, which finished many champions including Am. and Can. Ch. Oudenarde Sea Hark, exported to Betty Hyslop; Uniquecottage Kennels of Mrs. J. G. Parker-Tucker, which produced over 30 English champions who have won many CCs. There have been an exceptional number of dedi-cated Cairn breeders in the British Isles whose dogs have been well known not only in their own country but also throughout North America.

THE CAIRN TERRIER IN NORTH AMERICA

The Cairn Terrier's history in America followed the history of the breed in Great Britain by only a few years. In 1913 the first Cairns were imported to the United States by Mrs. Henry Price of California from Mrs. Fleming's Out of the West Kennels. Sandy Peter Out of the West was the first and only Cairn registered with the American Kennel Club (AKC) in 1913.

By 1917 there were 32 regis-trations and, by December of that

BREED RECOGNITION

Mrs. Campbell, when she was struggling to see the breed recognized, wrote in a letter, "It seems a pity that this breed, of which so many people are fond, should be allowed to die out. There is nothing like showing a dog to keep up the characteristics of the breed. I propose to endeavour to have them recognised as 'Old Breed' or 'Sporting Skye Terrier'."

relying upon their homebreds.

Between 1913 and 1930, imports from Great Britain accounted for two-thirds of the American champions. The Cairn continued its successful and winning ways in America throughout the 1930s and 1940s in spite of the Great Depression and World War II.

Shagbark Kennel of Helen Hunt in Connecticut began in the 1930s and had over 30 champions. In the 1950s Miss Hunt had five generations of home-

year, the Cairn Terrier Club of America made it as the ninth in the Terrier Group to become a member of the AKC. Mrs. Price became an active breeder and exhibitor through the early 1940s. She had a life-long interest in the breed and served on the board of the national club. Mrs. Byron Rogers, a Cairn and Sealyham fancier and also a board member, imported many Cairns from England and wrote the first book on the breed. Mrs. C. Groverman Ellis of Killybracken Kennels added Cairns to her kennel of Irish Wolfhounds in the 1930s. She produced nearly 40 champions in addition to putting obedience degrees on many of her Cairns. Ch. Tam Glen of Killybracken may still be one of the only Cairns with a tracking degree. The owners usually showed their own dogs and purchased few outside dogs,

A distinguished pair, Mousie and Victory, seen with the Hon. Lady Morrison Bell and her daughter, Miss Shelagh Morrison Bell, from the famed family of the 1920s.

breds in her kennel. Mrs. R. T. Allen owned the Craigdhu Kennels in Illinois; they were breeders of top Cairns for 45 years. Mrs. Betty Stone's Caithness Kennels imported several dogs from England and bred Ch. Caithness Rufus, who won the Cairn Terrier Club of America national specialty show in 1964 from the Puppy Class. Rufus sired more than 25 champions and was retired from the show ring to make way for his son, Ch. Cairnwoods Golden Boy. Mrs. Stone died in the mid-1970s.

Joe and Betty Marcum's, Cairmar Kennels of Mississippi have been very successful, producing Group winners and

THE CAIRN AND THE WESTIE

The Cairn Terrier and the West Highland White Terrier closely resemble each other. The early Cairn breeders were very careful not to keep Cairn puppies that had any white in their coats; any puppies that did have white were culled at birth. On the other hand, the breeders of the white terriers made certain that their dogs were *completely* white. Interbreeding of the two breeds continued until 1917 when the American Kennel Club stated that no Cairn could be registered if there was a Westie cross within the first three generations. The Kennel Club of England followed suit shortly after.

Best in Show dogs. Two of their dogs, who came from Mrs. Stone's Caithness Kennels, were Ch. Caithness Barnabas, sire of 31 champions, and Caithness Captie Periwinkle, dam of 7 champions. The Marcums have built their kennel on the strength of their bitches, which proves that "good-producing bitches make a good kennel." Mrs. Marcum is still an active figure in the breed and has written an excellent book on the Cairn Terrier.

The Wolfpit Kennels, started in the 1930s by Mr. and Mrs. Taylor Coleman and their daughter Lydia Coleman Hutchinson, have produced over 115 champions. Their top winner was Ch. Cairnwood's Quince (Ch. Cairnwoods Golden Boy ex Caithness Gracenote) who won numerous Groups, an all-breed Best in Show and the national specialty in 1971, 1972, 1973 and again in 1980 at the age of 12. He was a top-producing sire of the breed, producing over 50 champions. Ch. Caithness Rufus was the key dog in his pedigree. Another top stud dog is Ch. Caledonian Berry of Wolfpit, winner of many specialty shows, 5 all-breed Bests in Show and sire of over 30 champions. Mrs. Coleman is a well-known terrier judge in the United States.

One breeder who should be considered a North American

breeder rather than a Canadian breeder was Mrs. Betty Hyslop of Cairndania Kennels in Ontario, Canada. Mrs. Hyslop's influence throughout North America lasted well over sixty years until her death in the late 1990s. She was a well-known figure at dog shows in both the US and Canada, and the Cairndania dogs were campaigned throughout both countries.

She purchased her first Cairn in 1928 from England and imported and bred dogs through the years, often showing them herself to the top spot. She thrice won the Terrier Group at the Westminster Kennel Club show, America's most prestigious dog show. Every decade has seen great dogs from out of this kennel. Ch. Redletter Mc Ruffie won the national specialty 3 times and sired 25 champions. All-breed Bests in Show were won in the 1960s by Ch. Cairndania Mc Brigand's Holbris, Ch. Uniquecottage Mr. Bradshaw and Ch. Cairndania Mc Brigand's Brigery, sire of 27 champions. Ch. Redletter Miss Splinters, imported by Mrs. Hyslop, was shown 60 times and defeated in the breed only once. The number of Best in Show winners and champions has been considerable, and the North American Cairn fancy was fortunate to have had such a supporter of the breed—one who bred and

VERE TEMPLE

imported great dogs for so many decades.

In the 1960s Cairns were exported to Japan, France, Sweden, Finland, Australia, Denmark and South Africa. Australia and Sweden have been breeding excellent Cairns for many years. The Cairn Terrier, in around 100 years, has become a very beloved breed. It continues to be in good hands with excellent breeders in America and around the world, and the future of the breed is indeed bright.

A special drawing by Vere Temple, which was entitled "Cairn Companions," came with the following caption: "These jolly fellows hailing from the North make happy subjects for the artist's pen...and Miss Temple's pen is always skillful."

CHARACTERISTICS OF THE
CAIRN TERRIER

The Cairn Terrier is a wonderful little dog! He's cute, is compact in size, has personality-plus and is an active dog. Some terriers, like the Cairn, are "below the knee" in height, but in spite of their size, all terriers are masculine dogs and do not show any sign of timidity or shyness. These are busy dogs, on their toes and ready for action!

Have you investigated the responsibilities of owning a Cairn? Or any dog for that matter? The long-haired Dachshund is smaller and usually less active than a Cairn Terrier. Cairns are energetic and always busy.

If you are looking for a sedentary lap dog, this will not be the breed for you.

The Cairn has a very steady disposition and fits in well with family life, whether it be in a large country house or a studio apartment in the city. He gets along well with children and will accept strangers once he has had a chance to look them over. He's a cocky dog who may not go out and start a fight, but he will surely stand his ground when pushed. This is not a dog who will lie about the house trying to keep his master or mistress happy. He has been bred as a hunter, a dog to go after vermin, and he can be ready to work at the drop of a "rat."

Common characteristics of all terriers are their desire to work with great enthusiasm and courage. They all have large and powerful teeth for the size of their bodies; they have keen hearing and excellent eyesight. No matter for how many generations they have been bred, the purpose for which the breed was intended will remain with the dog.

The Cairn Terrier is a versatile dog and a great house dog and companion. If you like to work

OH, TOTO!

In 1899 Frank Baum wrote *The Emerald City*, later retitled as *The Wonderful Wizard of Oz*. At the turn of the century, Baum's stories were adapted into a popular musical on Broadway. Some years later, the movie musical opened in 1939, with a completely new score by Harold Arlen and the 16-year-old Judy Garland starring as Dorothy. Her dog, Toto, was played by a rather scruffy Cairn Terrier. Dorothy, Toto and the cast of the movie are all still dearly beloved characters in this Hollywood classic.

with your dog, you will find the Cairn to be a happy and willing participant in whatever area you choose, be it obedience work, agility, therapy, flyball or, of course, best of all, going-to-ground activities. This is a smart little dog that likes to please, to keep busy and to be challenged. Give him any job that requires a bit of brain activity on his part and he will be a happy camper. Of course, because of his intelligence, it is best to establish very early on who is the head of the household and the very basic obedience lessons are always a good idea. If you are a first-time

You should never buy a dog for his color alone. If all other desirable characteristics about the puppy are the same (size, temperament, breeding, etc.) , then your choice of color is valid.

The Cairn is a smart little dog that likes to please. Because of his intelligence, it is best to establish early on who is the head of the household.

Cairns, as with other terriers, can be a challenge in the obedience ring. Terriers are not easy breeds to work with in obedience as with their intelligence and independent spirit they can sometimes be more trying to train than had been anticipated. You will see Golden Retrievers, Poodles and Border Collies in abundance in obedience classes as these are breeds that are easy to work with. Not only are they intelligent, but more importantly they have a willingness to please their master. The terrier is easily distracted and busy but he is an intelligent dog and he does respond to training. Of course, when training a smart and independent dog, the handler will often learn humility while the dog is learning his sits and stays. The Cairn is a quick, alert and intelligent dog and he likes his owner to be his equal.

dog owner, you must be aware of your responsibility toward your new friend. Either keep your dog on a leash or in your fenced yard. Your Cairn, if loose and trotting along your side, will spot a squirrel across a busy street and his instincts will react quickly. Be mindful, for he will dart across the street, never minding the traffic. Therefore, some rudimentary obedience training should be in line so your friend will sit when asked to, come when called and, in general, act like a little gentleman.

WORKING TRIALS FOR TERRIERS

The American Working Terrier Association offers a Certificate of Gameness at sanctioned trials. A dog must enter a 10-foot-long tunnel buried in the ground, which includes one right-angle turn. Once in the tunnel, he must reach his prey in 30 seconds. Working trials are held throughout the country and open to all terriers.

Cairns make great, loving pets, but they should not be allowed to chew on babies' pacifiers, nor should they lick or kiss the baby, for health reasons.

If you plan to become a Cairn Terrier owner, you should be aware that this is a breed that will require some specialized grooming. Grooming will be more extensive than with a smooth-coated dog but far less detailed work than with either a Scottish or Bedlington Terrier.

HEALTH CONSIDERATIONS

Cairn Terriers are very healthy dogs, as are most terriers. However, there are health problems in most breeds of dogs and the Cairn Terrier is no exception. The potential and new owner should be aware of these problems. Do remember to buy

THE CARING CAIRN

Do you want to live longer? If you like to volunteer, it is wonderful if you can take your Cairn to a nursing home once a week for an hour or two. The elder community loves to have a dog to visit with and often your dog will bring a bit of companionship to someone who is either lonely or who may be somewhat detached from the world. You will not only be bringing happiness to someone else but you will also be keeping your little dog busy—and we haven't even mentioned the fact that they have discovered that volunteering helps to increase your longevity!

your puppy from a reputable breeder and ask the breeder if any of these health problems are in his line. It pays to ask questions before getting attached to a lovable Cairn baby.

CRANIOMANDIBULAR OSTEOPATHY (CMO)

CMO is a fairly rare disease found in Westies, Scotties and Cairns. It is apparently a hereditary disease although the exact pattern of inheritance is not known. There is a calcification of the joint between the lower jaw and the skull along with a multiplication in growth of bone cells. It usually occurs between four to seven months and it must not be confused with a teething problem or with cancer. Puppies who have this disease will have difficulty in opening their mouths. Diagnosis is made by x-ray, and cortisone and

homeopathic remedies have been used with good results. This is a very painful disease for the dog.

GLOBOID-CELL LEUKODYSTROPHY (KRABBE'S DISEASE)

Krabbe's disease is inherited as a simple autosomal recessive defect. It is known to be in both the Cairn and the West Highland White Terrier. At about four months of age, the infected dog will show lack of coordination and hind leg stiffness. This is a lethal blood disorder for which there is no cure or treatment available.

CEREBELLAR HYPOPLASIA

This condition is also passed as a recessive gene, though it is quite unusual and is sometimes reported in cats, related to panleukopenia virus before birth.

Though no conclusive study is available, the condition has been reported in Cairn Terriers.

OTHER CONCERNS

Additionally, hip dysplasia, the most common of orthopedic problems in dogs, as well as myasthenia gravis, a muscle disorder, inguinal hernias, hemophilia and inhalant allergies have been documented in the breed.

Although these health problems may look daunting, Cairns are considered to be a healthy breed. The problems mentioned are in the breed and a buyer should be aware of them. These diseases are rare and only turn up on the rare occasion. Do not be turned away from the breed but do be aware that if the breeder of your puppy is reputable and aware of these problems, he will be doing his utmost to keep them out of his line.

Williams Haynes wrote in 1925, "The terrier owner is a 'lucky devil' for his dogs do not, as a rule, spend a great deal of time in the hospital. All members of the terrier family, from the giant of the race, the Airedale, way down to little Scottie, owe a big debt to Nature for having blessed them with remarkably robust constitutions. Even when really sick, they make wonderfully rapid recoveries."

While not all Cairns are obedience and agility performers, all Cairns welcome a game of fetch with their favorite chew device. Do not use a small ball that can be accidentally swallowed.

BREED STANDARD FOR THE

CAIRN TERRIER

Each breed approved by the American Kennel Club has a standard that provides a mental picture of what the specific breed should look like. All reputable breeders strive to produce animals that will meet the requirements of the standard. Many breeds were developed for a specific purpose, e.g., hunting, retrieving, going to ground, coursing, guarding and herding. The terriers were all bred to go to ground and to pursue vermin. In addition to having dogs that look like proper Cairn Terriers, the standard assures that the Cairn will have the personality, disposition and intelligence that are sought after in the breed.

Standards were originally written by experts who had a love and a concern for the breed. They knew that the essential characteristics of the Cairn Terrier were unlike those of any other breed and that care must be taken that these characteristics were maintained through the generations.

As time progressed and breeders became more aware that certain areas of the dog needed a better description or more definition, breeders would meet together and work out a new standard. However, standards for any breed are never changed on a whim and serious study and exchange between breeders takes place before any move is made. The Cairn Terrier Club of America is responsible for any alteration to the standard, which are then approved by the membership and sent to the American Kennel Club.

SCOTCH TERRIERS

The dogs originally known as Scotch terriers include the Cairn, Scottish and Westie. The Scottish Terrier is a heavy-boned, muscular dog whose colors are black, brindle and wheaten. He has a long muzzle and a longer ear compared to the West Highland White or the Cairn Terrier. The Westie is much lighter in weight and bone than the Scottie, he has a shorter, broad muzzle and his ears are smaller than a Scottie's. His color is white. The Westie is some sturdier than the Cairn, broader in skull and wider in ear carriage. The Cairn has a profuse harsh outer coat with a soft, close undercoat. His coat is shown in a neatened condition rather than in a tailored jacket as are the Scottie and Westie coats.

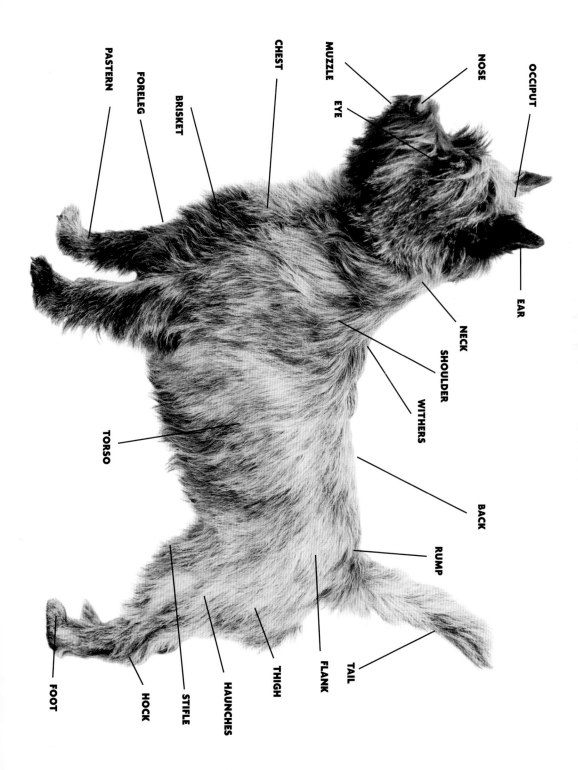

PASTERN

FORELEG

BRISKET

CHEST

MUZZLE

EYE

NOSE

OCCIPUT

EAR

NECK

SHOULDER

WITHERS

TORSO

BACK

RUMP

FOOT

HOCK

STIFLE

HAUNCHES

THIGH

FLANK

TAIL

THE AMERICAN KENNEL CLUB STANDARD FOR THE CAIRN TERRIER

General Appearance: That of an active, game, hardy, small working terrier of the short-legged class; very free in its movements, strongly but not heavily built, standing well forward on its forelegs, deep in the ribs, well coupled with strong hindquarters and presenting a well-proportioned build with a medium length of back, having a hard, weather-resisting coat; head shorter and wider than any other terrier and well furnished with hair giving a general foxy expression.

Head: *Skull* Broad in proportion to length with a decided stop and well furnished with hair on the top of the head, which may be somewhat softer than the body coat. *Muzzle* Strong but not too long or heavy. *Teeth* Large, mouth neither overshot nor undershot. *Nose* Black. *Eyes* Set wide apart,

Incorrect head and ear set. Head is too thin and ears are too close together.

rather sunken, with shaggy eyebrows, medium in size, hazel or dark hazel in color, depending on body color, with a keen terrier expression. *Ears* Small, pointed, well carried erectly, set wide apart on the side of the head. Free from long hairs.

Incorrect muzzle—too long.   Correct muzzle.

Correct head.

Shoulders, Legs and Feet: A sloping shoulder, medium length of leg, good but not too heavy bone; forelegs should not be out at elbows, and be perfectly straight, but forefeet may be slightly turned

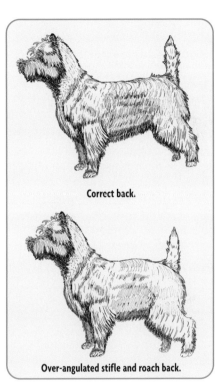

Correct back.

Over-angulated stifle and roach back.

Tail: In proportion to head, well furnished with hair but not feathery. Carried gaily but must not curl over back. Set on at back level.

Body: Well-muscled, strong, active body with well-sprung, deep ribs, coupled to strong hindquarters, with a level back of medium length, giving an impression of strength and activity without heaviness.

Correct tail.

Incorrect tail, due to curl.

Incorrect tail, due to high set and feathering.

out. Forefeet larger than hind feet. Legs must be covered with hard hair. Pads should be thick and strong and dog should stand well up on its feet.

Coat: Hard and weather-resistant. Must be double-coated with profuse harsh outer coat and short, soft, close furry undercoat.

Color: May be of any color except white. Dark ears, muzzle and tail tip are desirable.

Ideal Size: Involves the weight, the height at the withers and the length of body. Weight for bitches, 13 pounds; for dogs, 14 pounds. Height at the withers: bitches, 9.5 inches; dogs, 10 inches. Length of body from 14.25 to 15 inches from the front of the chest to back of hindquarters. The dog must be of balanced proportions and appear neither leggy nor too low to ground; and neither too short nor too long in body. Weight and measurements are for matured dogs at two years of age. Older dogs may weigh slightly in excess and growing dogs may be under these weights and measurements.

Condition: Dogs should be shown in good hard flesh, well muscled and neither too fat or thin. Should be in full good coat with plenty of head furnishings, be clean, combed, brushed and tidied up on ears, tail, feet and general outline. Should move freely and easily on a loose lead, should not cringe on being handled, should stand up on their toes and show with marked terrier characteristics.

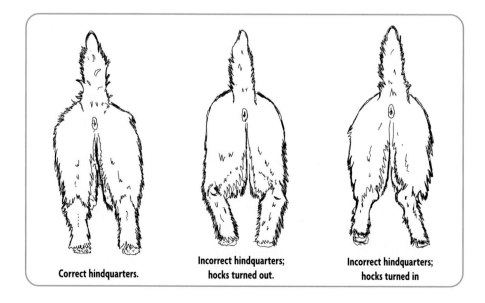

Correct hindquarters.   Incorrect hindquarters; hocks turned out.   Incorrect hindquarters; hocks turned in

The Cairn's coat is hard and weather-resistant with a profuse harsh outer coat.

FAULTS

1. *Skull* Too narrow in skull.
2. *Muzzle* Too long and heavy a foreface; mouth overshot or undershot.
3. *Eyes* Too large, prominent, yellow, and ringed are all objectionable.
4. *Ears* Too large, round at points, set too close together, set too high on the head; heavily covered with hair.
5. *Legs and Feet* Too light or too heavy bone. Crooked forelegs or out at elbow. Thin, ferrety feet; feet let down on the heel or too open and spread. Too high or too low on the leg.
6. *Body* Too short back and compact a body, hampering quickness of movement and turning ability. Too long, weedy and snaky a body, giving an impression of weakness. Tail set on too low. Back not level.
7. *Coat* Open coats, blousy coats, too short or dead coats, lack of sufficient undercoat, lack of head furnishings, lack of hard hair on the legs. Silkiness or curliness. A slight wave permissible.
8. *Nose* Flesh or light-colored nose.
9. *Color* White on chest, feet or other parts of body.

Approved May 10, 1938

CAIRN TERRIER

WHERE TO BEGIN

If you are convinced that the Cairn Terrier is the ideal dog for you, it's time to learn about where to find a puppy and what to look for. Locating a litter of Cairn Terriers should not present a problem for the new owner. You should inquire about breeders in your area who enjoy a good reputation in the breed. You are looking for an established breeder with outstanding dog ethics and a strong commitment to the breed. New owners should have as many questions as they have doubts. An established breeder is indeed the one to answer your four million questions and make you comfortable with your choice of the Cairn Terrier. An established breeder will sell you a puppy at a fair price if, and only if, the breeder determines that you are a suitable, worthy owner of his dogs. An established breeder can be relied upon for advice, no matter what time of day or night. A reputable breeder will accept a puppy back, without questions, should you decide that this not the right dog for you.

When choosing a breeder, reputation is much more important than convenience of location. Do not be impressed by breeders who run brag advertisements in the presses about their stupendous champions and top producers. The real quality breeders are quiet and unassuming. You hear about them at the dog shows and trials, by word of mouth. You may be well advised to avoid the novice who lives only a few miles away. The local novice breeder, trying so hard to get rid of that first litter of puppies, is more than accommodating and anxious to sell you one. That breeder will charge you as much as any established breeder. The novice breeder isn't going to interrogate you and your family about your intentions with the puppy, the environment and

A Cairn Terrier and an Irish Wolfhound. The choice between these two breeds is much simpler than choosing between breeds that are closely related like Scottish Terriers, West Highland White Terriers and Skye Terriers, all of whom are closely associated with the development of the Cairn.

reputable breeder who doesn't live on the other side of the country (or in a different country). The American Kennel Club (AKC) is able to recommend breeders of quality Cairn Terriers, as can any local all-breed club or Cairn Terrier club. Potential owners are encouraged to attend dog shows to see the Cairn Terriers in action, to meet the handlers firsthand and to get an idea of what Cairn training you can provide, etc. That breeder will be nowhere to be found when your poorly bred, badly adjusted four-pawed monster starts to growl and spit up at midnight or eat the family cat!

While health considerations in the Cairn Terrier are not nearly as daunting as in most other breeds, socialization is always of immense importance. While personality within a breed should be rather consistent, temperament can vary from line to line and socialization is the first and best way to encourage a proper, stable personality.

Choosing a breeder is an important first step in dog ownership. Fortunately, the majority of Cairn Terrier breeders are devoted to the breed and its well-being. New owners should have little problem finding a

ARE YOU PREPARED?

Unfortunately, when a puppy is bought by someone who does not take into consideration the time and attention that dog ownership requires, it is the puppy who suffers when he is either abandoned or placed in a shelter by a frustrated owner. So all of the "homework" you do in preparation for your pup's arrival will benefit you both. The more informed you are, the more you will know what to expect and the better equipped you will be to handle the ups and downs of raising a puppy. Hopefully, everyone in the household is willing to do his part in raising and caring for the pup. The anticipation of owning a dog often brings a lot of promises from excited family members: "I will walk him every day," "I will feed him," "I will house-train him," etc., but these things take time and effort, and promises can easily be forgotten once the novelty of the new pet has worn off.

committed to the breeder whom you've selected, then you will wait (and hope for an early arrival!). If not, you may have to resort to your second- or third-

This Cairn puppy won first prize.

Terriers look like outside a photographer's lens. Provided you approach the handlers when they are not terribly busy with the dogs, most are more than willing to answer questions, recommend breeders and give advice.

Visit dog shows to see the Cairns up close and to meet the breeders and exhibitors.

Now that you have contacted and met a breeder or two and made your choice about which breeder is best suited to your needs, it's time to visit the litter. Keep in mind that many top breeders have waiting lists. Sometimes new owners have to wait as long as two years for a puppy. If you are really

choice breeder. Don't be too anxious, however. If the breeder doesn't have any waiting list, or any customers, there is probably a good reason.

Since you are likely to be choosing a Cairn Terrier as a pet dog and not a show dog, you simply should select a pup that is friendly and attractive. Cairn Terriers generally have small litters, averaging five puppies, so selection is limited once you have located a desirable litter. While the basic structure of the breed has little variation, the temperament may present trouble in certain strains. Beware of the shy or overly aggressive puppy, be especially conscious of the nervous Cairn Terrier pup. Don't let sentiment or emotion trap you into buying the runt of the litter.

The gender of your puppy is largely a matter of personal taste,

TEMPERAMENT COUNTS

Your selection of a good puppy can be determined by your needs. A show potential or a good pet? It is your choice. Every puppy, however, should be of good temperament. Although show-quality puppies are bred and raised with emphasis on physical conformation, responsible breeders strive for equally good temperament. Do not buy from a breeder who concentrates solely on physical beauty at the expense of personality.

especially when choosing a pet, since you will not be breeding the dog. Regardless of gender, all Cairn pups should be lively and alert. In Cairn Terriers, the difference in size is noticeable but slight, males being larger.

Breeders commonly allow visitors to see the litter by around the fifth or sixth week, and puppies leave for their new homes between the eighth and tenth week. Breeders who permit their puppies to leave early are more interested in your money than their puppies' well-being. Puppies need to learn the rules of the trade from their dam, and most dams continue teaching the

When visiting a dog show, approach the handlers after they have completed their work in the ring. Many will be happy to talk to you about their breed.

pups manners and dos and don'ts until around the eighth week. Breeders spend significant amounts of time with the Cairn Terrier toddlers so that they are able to interact with the "other species," i.e., humans. Given the long history that dogs and humans have, bonding between the two species is natural but must be nurtured. A well-bred, well-socialized Cairn Terrier pup wants nothing more than to be near you and please you.

Always check the bite of your selected puppy to be sure that it is neither overshot or undershot. This may not be too noticeable on a young puppy but it is still important to check for overall soundness.

COMMITMENT OF OWNERSHIP
After considering all of these factors, you have most likely already made some very important decisions about

PEDIGREE VS. REGISTRATION CERTIFICATE

Too often new owners are confused between these two important documents. Your puppy's pedigree, essentially a family tree, is a written record of a dog's genealogy of three generations or more. The pedigree will show you the names as well as performance titles of all dogs in your pup's background. Your breeder must provide you with a registration application, with his part properly filled out. You must complete the application and send it to the AKC with the proper fee. Every puppy must come from a litter that has been AKC-registered by the breeder, born in the US and from a sire and dam that are also registered with the AKC.

The seller must provide you with complete records to identify the puppy. The AKC requires that the seller provide the buyer with the following: breed; sex, color and markings; date of birth; litter number (when available); names and registration numbers of the parents; breeder's name; and date sold or delivered.

selecting your puppy. You have chosen the Cairn Terrier, which means that you have decided which characteristics you want in a dog and what type of dog will best fit into your family and lifestyle. If you have selected a breeder, you have gone a step further—you have done your research and found a responsible, conscientious person who breeds quality Cairn Terrier and who should be a reliable source of help as you and your puppy adjust to life together. If you have observed a litter in action, you have

PET INSURANCE

Just like you can insure your car, your house and your own health, you likewise can insure your dog's health. Investigate a pet insurance policy by talking to your vet. Depending on the age of your dog, the breed and the kind of coverage you desire, your policy can be very affordable. Most policies cover accidental injuries, poisoning and thousands of medical problems and illnesses, including cancers. Some carriers also offer routine care and immunization coverage.

Here's a growing, sleepy litter of Cairns. You must observe the dynamics of the "pack" and learn about each pup's individual personality, then choose the one that best suits you.

obtained a firsthand look at the dynamics of a puppy "pack" and, thus, you should learn about each pup's individual personality—perhaps you have even found one that particularly appeals to you.

However, even if you have not yet found the Cairn Terrier puppy of your dreams, observing pups will help you learn to recognize certain behavior and to determine what a pup's behavior indicates about his temperament. You will be able to pick out which pups are the leaders, which ones are less outgoing, which ones are confident, which ones are shy, playful, friendly, aggressive, etc. Equally as important, you will learn to recognize what a healthy pup should look and act like. All of these things will help you in your search, and when you find

ARE YOU A FIT OWNER?

If the breeder from whom you are buying a puppy asks you a lot of personal questions, do not be insulted. Such a breeder wants to be sure that you will be a fit provider for his puppy.

Observing pups will help you to learn to recognize certain behavior. By the third or fourth week, the pups' personalities begin to emerge.

the Cairn Terrier that was meant for you, you will know it!

Researching your breed, selecting a responsible breeder and observing as many pups as possible are all important steps on the way to dog ownership. It may seem like a lot of effort...and you

have not even brought the pup home yet! Remember, though, you cannot be too careful when it comes to deciding on the type of dog you want and finding out about your prospective pup's background. Buying a puppy is not—or should not be—just another whimsical purchase. This is one instance in which you actually do get to choose your own family! You may be thinking that buying a puppy should be fun—it should not be so serious and so much work. Keep in mind that your puppy is not a cuddly stuffed toy or decorative ornament, but a creature that will

At four weeks of age, the puppies are still too young to be removed from their mother. Potential owners are well advised to meet the dam of the litter to evaluate her appearance and temperament.

become a real member of your family. You will come to realize that, while buying a puppy is a pleasurable and exciting endeavor, it is not something to be taken lightly. Relax...the fun will start when the pup comes home!

Always keep in mind that a puppy is nothing more than a baby in a furry disguise...a baby who is virtually helpless in a human world and who trusts his owner for fulfillment of his basic needs for survival. In addition to

YOUR SCHEDULE...

If you lead an erratic, unpredictable life, with daily or weekly changes in your work requirements, consider the problems of owning a puppy. The new puppy has to be fed regularly, socialized (loved, petted, handled, introduced to other people) and, most importantly, allowed to go outdoors for house-training. As the dog gets older, he can be more tolerant of deviations in his feeding and relief schedule.

As adorable as a teddy, your Cairn still requires supervision. Cairns can tear stuffed animals apart in no time, perhaps swallowing bits that may cause serious health problems. Only use toys made especially for dogs.

food, water and shelter, your pup needs care, protection, guidance and love. If you are not prepared to commit to this, then you are not prepared to own a dog.

"Wait a minute," you say. "How hard could this be? All of my neighbors own dogs and they seem to be doing just fine. Why should I have to worry about all of this?" Well, you should not worry about it; in fact, you will probably find that once your Cairn Terrier pup gets used to his new home, he will fall into his place in the family quite naturally. But it never hurts to emphasize the commitment of dog ownership. With some time and patience, it is really not too difficult to raise a curious and exuberant Cairn Terrier pup to be a well-adjusted and well-mannered adult dog—a dog that could be your most loyal friend.

PREPARING PUPPY'S PLACE
Researching your breed and finding a breeder are only two aspects of the "homework" you

> **QUALITY FOOD**
> The cost of food must be mentioned. All dogs need a good-quality food with an adequate supply of protein to develop their bones and muscles properly. Most dogs are not picky eaters but, unless fed properly, can quickly succumb to skin problems.

will have to do before bringing your Cairn Terrier puppy home. You will also have to prepare your home and family for the new addition. Much as you would prepare a nursery for a newborn baby, you will need to designate a place in your home that will be the puppy's own. How you prepare your home will depend on how much freedom the dog will be allowed. Whatever you decide, you must ensure that he has a place that he can "call his own."

When you bring your new puppy into your home, you are bringing him into what will become his home as well. Obviously, you did not buy a puppy so that he could take over your house, but in order for a puppy to grow into a stable, well-adjusted dog, he has to feel comfortable in his surroundings.

Remember, he is leaving the warmth and security of his mother and littermates, as well as the familiarity of the only place he has ever known, so it is important to make his transition as easy as possible. By preparing a place in your home for the puppy, you are making him feel as welcome as possible in a strange new place. It should not take him long to get used to it, but the sudden shock of being transplanted is somewhat traumatic for a young pup. Imagine how a small child would feel in the same situation—that is how your puppy must be feeling. It is up to you to reassure him and to let him know, "Little fellow, you are going to like it here!"

WHAT YOU SHOULD BUY

CRATE

To someone unfamiliar with the use of crates in dog training, it may seem like punishment to shut a dog in a crate, but this is not the case at all. Most breeders advocate crate training for show puppies as well as pet puppies. Crates are not cruel—crates have many humane and highly effective uses in dog care and training. The crate offers the dog a sense of structure and regularity in a variety of ways. For example, crate training is a very popular and very successful housebreaking method. A crate

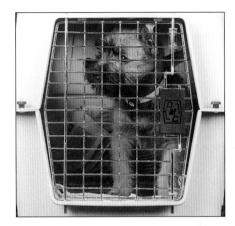

This medium-size crate is sufficient for a puppy or a full-grown Cairn Terrier. Once acclimated, your dog will be perfectly happy and secure in his crate.

can keep your dog safe during travel and, perhaps most importantly, a crate provides your dog with a place of his own in your home. It serves as a "doggie bedroom" of sorts—your Cairn Terrier can curl up in his crate when he wants to sleep or when he just needs a break. Many dogs sleep in their crates overnight. When lined with soft bedding and a favorite toy, a crate becomes a

TIME TO GO HOME

Breeders rarely release puppies until they are eight to ten weeks of age. This is an acceptable age for most breeds of dog, excepting Toy breeds, which are not released until around 12 weeks, given their petite sizes. If a breeder has a puppy that is 12 weeks of age or older, he is likely well socialized and house-trained. Be sure that he is otherwise healthy before deciding to take him home.

PHOTO COURTESY OF DOSKOCIL.

two most popular types: wire or fiberglass. There are advantages and disadvantages to each type. For example, a wire crate is more open, allowing the air to flow through and affording the dog a view of what is going on around him, while a fiberglass crate is sturdier. Both can double as travel crates, providing protection for the dog. The size of the crate is another thing to consider. A medium-sized crate will be fine for a Cairn Terrier pup or adult.

BEDDING

A soft crate pad in the dog's crate will help the dog feel more at home and you may also like to put in a small blanket. This will take the place of the leaves, twigs, etc., that the pup would use in the wild to make a den; the pup can make his own "burrow" in the crate. Although your pup is far removed from his den-making ancestors, the denning instinct is still a part of his genetic makeup. Second, until you bring your pup home, he has been sleeping amid the warmth of his dam and litter-mates, and while a blanket is not the same as a warm, breathing body, it still provides heat and something with which to snuggle. You will want to wash your pup's bedding frequently in case he has an accident in his crate, and replace or remove any blanket that becomes ragged and starts to fall apart.

Your local pet shop offers a variety of crates from which to choose. The mid-size crate is desirable for the Cairn.

cozy pseudo-den for your dog. Like his ancestors, he too will seek out the comfort and retreat of a den—you just happen to be providing him with something a little more luxurious than his early ancestors enjoyed.

As far as purchasing a crate, the type that you buy is up to you. It will most likely be one of the

Toys

Toys are a must for dogs of all ages, especially for curious playful pups. Puppies are the "children" of the dog world, and what child does not love toys? Chew toys provide enjoyment to both dog and owner—your dog will enjoy playing with his favorite toys, while you will enjoy the fact that they distract him from your expensive shoes and leather sofa. Puppies love to chew; in fact, chewing is a physical need for pups as they are teething, and everything looks appetizing! The full range of your

Wire crates are popular for use in the home. These crates provide better ventilation and visibility for your Cairn.

possessions—from slippers to Oriental rug—are fair game in the eyes of a teething pup. Puppies are not all that discerning when it comes to finding something to literally "sink their teeth into"— everything tastes great!

Squeaky toys are very popular, but must be avoided for the Cairn Terrier. Perhaps a squeaky toy can be used as an aid in training, but not for free play. If a pup "disembowels" one of these, the small plastic squeaker inside can be dangerous if swallowed. Monitor the condition of all your pup's toys carefully and get rid of any that have been chewed to the point of becoming potentially dangerous.

Be careful of natural bones,

CRATE-TRAINING TIPS

During crate training, you should partition off the section of the crate in which the pup stays. If he is given too big an area, this will hinder your training efforts. Crate training is based on the fact that a dog does not like to soil his sleeping quarters, so it is ineffective to keep a pup in an area that is so big that he can eliminate in one end and get far enough away from it to sleep. Also, you want to make the crate den-like for the pup. Blankets and a favorite toy will make the crate cozy for the small pup; as he grows, you may want to evict some of his "roommates" to make more room. It will take some coaxing at first, but be patient. Given some time to get used to it, your pup will adapt to his new home-within-a-home quite nicely.

Your pet store has a variety of enjoyable toys for your pup. Try out one or two of these on your Cairn.

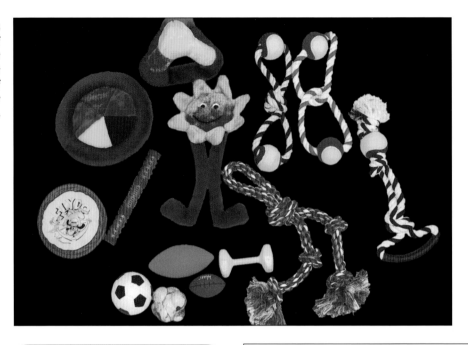

TOYS, TOYS, TOYS!

With a big variety of dog toys available, and so many that look like they would be a lot of fun for a dog, be careful in your selection. It is amazing what a set of puppy teeth can do to an innocent-looking toy, so, obviously, safety is a major consideration. Be sure to choose the most durable products that you can find. Hard nylon bones and toys are a safe bet, and many of them are offered in different scents and flavors that will be sure to capture your dog's attention. It is always fun to play a game of fetch with your dog, and there are balls and flying discs that are specially made to withstand dog teeth.

which have a tendency to splinter into sharp, dangerous pieces. Also be careful of rawhide, which can turn into pieces that are easy to swallow or into a mushy mess on your carpet.

LEAD

A nylon lead is probably the best option as it is the most resistant to puppy teeth should your pup take a liking to chewing on his lead. Of course, this is a habit that should be nipped in the bud, but if your pup likes to chew on his lead he has a very slim chance of being able to chew through the strong nylon. Nylon leads are also lightweight, which is good for a

If you want your dog to be near you during certain parts of the day or night, get him an easily movable bed and place it close to where you are sitting.

young Cairn Terrier who is just getting used to the idea of walking on a lead. For everyday walking and safety purposes, the nylon lead is a good choice. As your pup grows up and gets used to walking on the lead, you may want to purchase a flexible lead. These leads allow you to extend the length to give the dog a broader area to explore or to shorten the length to keep the dog close to you. Of course there are special leads for training purposes, but these are not necessary for routine walks with your Cairn Terrier.

Pet shops offer dog toys that have been approved for their tear-resistance. Never offer a Cairn Terrier human toys that can be readily destroyed and swallowed.

COLLAR

Your pup should get used to wearing a collar all the time since you will want to attach his ID tags to it. Plus, you have to attach the lead to something! A lightweight nylon collar is a good choice;

A leash or lead is not a chew toy, and your Cairn has to learn that chewing on the leash is unacceptable behavior.

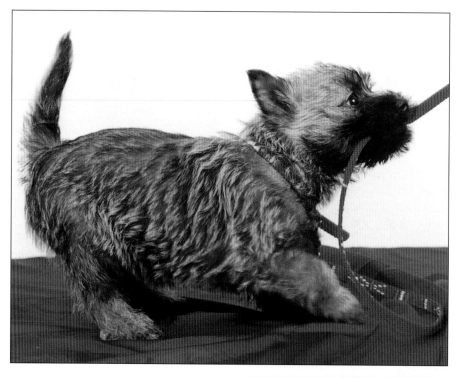

Your local pet shop will have a wide selection of leashes from which you can make a choice.

FINANCIAL RESPONSIBILITY

Grooming tools, collars, leashes, crate, dog beds and, of course, toys will be expenses to you when you first obtain your pup, and the cost will continue throughout your dog's lifetime. If your puppy damages or destroys your possessions (as most puppies surely will!) or something belonging to a neighbor, you can calculate additional expense. There is also flea and pest control, which every dog owner faces more than once. You must be able to handle the financial responsibility of owning a dog.

make sure that it fits snugly enough so that the pup cannot wriggle out of it, but is loose enough so that it will not be uncomfortably tight around the pup's neck. You should be able to fit a finger between the pup and the collar. It may take some time for your pup to get used to wearing the collar, but soon he will not even notice that it is there. Choke collars are made for training, and should never be left on the dog when not training.

FOOD AND WATER BOWLS

Your pup will need two bowls, one for food and one for water. You may want two sets of bowls, one for inside and one for outside, depending on where the dog will be fed and where he will be spending most of his time. Stainless steel or sturdy plastic bowls are popular choices. Plastic bowls are more chewable. Dogs tend not to chew on the steel variety, which can be sterilized. It is important to buy sturdy bowls since anything is in danger of being chewed by puppy teeth and you do not want your dog to be constantly chewing apart his bowl (for his safety and for your purse!).

CLEANING SUPPLIES

Until a pup is house-trained, you will be doing a lot of cleaning. Accidents will occur, which is okay in the beginning because the

Stainless steel bowls for water or food, as well as sturdy plastic bowls, are available at your pet store.

puppy does not know any better. All you can do is be prepared to clean up any "accidents." Old rags, paper towels, newspapers and a safe disinfectant are good to have on hand.

BEYOND THE BASICS

The items previously discussed are the bare necessities. You will find out what else you need as you go along—grooming supplies, flea/tick protection, baby gates to partition a room, etc. These things will vary depending on your situation but it is important that you have everything you need to feed and make your Cairn Terrier comfortable in his first few days at home.

The Cairn puppy should become accustomed to wearing a collar at all times. Be sure that his identification tags are securely fastened.

Your local pet shop sells an array of dishes and bowls for water and food.

It is your responsibility to clean up after your dog has relieved himself. Pet shops have various tools to assist in the cleanup job.

PHOTO COURTESY OF MIKKI PET PRODUCTS.

PUPPY-PROOFING YOUR HOME

Aside from making sure that your Cairn Terrier will be comfortable in your home, you also have to make sure that your home is safe for your Cairn Terrier. This means taking precautions that your pup will not get into anything he should not get into and that there is nothing within his reach that may harm him should he sniff it, chew it, inspect it, etc. This probably seems obvious since, while you are primarily concerned with your pup's safety, at the same time you do not want your belongings to be ruined. Breakables should be placed out of reach if your dog is to have full run of the house. If he is to be

CHOOSE AN APPROPRIATE COLLAR

The **BUCKLE COLLAR** is the standard collar used for everyday purposes. Be sure that you adjust the buckle on growing puppies. Check it every day. It can become too tight overnight! These collars can be made of leather or nylon. Attach your dog's identification tags to this collar.

The **CHOKE COLLAR** is designed for training. It is constructed of highly polished steel so that it slides easily through the stainless steel loop. The idea is that the dog controls the pressure around his neck and he will stop pulling if the collar becomes uncomfortable.

The **HALTER** is for a trained dog that has to be restrained to prevent running away, chasing a cat and the like. Considered the most humane of all collars, it is frequently used on smaller dogs on which collars are not comfortable.

A SAFE HOME

Scour your garage for potential puppy dangers. Remove weed killers, pesticides and antifreeze materials. Antifreeze is highly toxic and just a few drops can kill a puppy or an adult dog. The sweet taste attracts the animal, who will quickly consume it from the floor or pavement.

Never use cockroach or rodent poisons or plant fertilizers in any area accessible to the puppy. Avoid the use of toilet cleaners. Most dogs are born with "toilet-bowl sonar" and will take a drink if the lid is left open. Also keep the trash secured and out of reach.

limited to certain places within the house, keep any potentially dangerous items in the "off-limits" areas. An electrical cord can pose a danger should the puppy decide to taste it—and who is going to convince a pup that it would not make a great chew toy? Cords should be fastened tightly against the wall. If your dog is going to spend time in a crate, make sure that there is nothing near his crate that he can reach if he sticks his curious little nose or paws through the openings. Just as you would with a child, keep all household cleaners and chemicals where the pup cannot get to them.

It is also important to make sure that the outside of your home is safe. Of course your puppy should never be unsupervised, but a pup let loose in the yard will want to run and explore, and he should be granted that freedom. Do not let a fence give you a false sense of security; you would be surprised how crafty (and persistent) a dog can be in working out how to dig under and squeeze his way through small holes, or to jump or climb over a fence. The remedy is to make the fence high enough so that it really is impossible for your dog to get over it (about 6 feet should suffice), and well embedded into the ground. Be sure to repair or secure any gaps in the fence. Check the fence periodically to ensure that it is in good shape and make repairs as needed—a very determined pup, especially an "earth dog" like your Cairn Terrier, may return to the same spot to "work on it" until he is able to get through.

FIRST TRIP TO THE VET

You have picked out your puppy, and your home and family are ready. Now all you have to do is collect your Cairn Terrier from the breeder and the fun begins, right? Well...not so fast. Something else you need to prepare is your pup's first trip to the veterinarian. Perhaps the breeder can recommend someone in the area who specializes in Cairn Terriers, or maybe you know some other Cairn Terrier owners who can suggest a good vet. Either way, you should have an appointment arranged for your pup before you pick him up and plan on taking him for an examination before bringing him home.

The pup's first visit will consist of an overall examination to make sure that the pup does not have any problems that are not apparent to you. The veterinarian will also set up a schedule for the pup's vaccinations; the breeder will inform you of which ones the pup has already received and the vet can continue from there.

Sturdy chew toys are entertaining, healthful diversions for your Cairn puppy. This will keep your new puppy from chewing on forbidden objects, such as electrical cords.

formed. Gentle petting and soothing words should help console him, as well as just putting him down and letting him explore on his own (under your watchful eye, of course).

The pup may approach the family members or may busy

INTRODUCTION TO THE FAMILY

Everyone in the house will be excited about the puppy's coming home and will want to pet him and play with him, but it is best to keep the introductions low-key so as not to overwhelm the puppy. He is apprehensive already. It is the first time he has been separated from his mother and the breeder, and the ride to your home is likely the first time he has been in a car. The last thing you want to do is smother him, as this will only frighten him further. This is not to say that human contact is not extremely necessary at this stage, because this is the time when a connection between the pup and his human family is

NATURAL TOXINS

Examine your grass and landscaping before bringing your puppy home. Many varieties of plants have leaves, stems or flowers that are toxic if ingested, and you can depend on a curious puppy to investigate them.

If you see your dog carrying a piece of vegetation in his mouth, approach him in a quiet, disinterested manner, avoid eye contact, pet him and gradually remove the plant from his mouth. Alternatively, offer him a treat and maybe he'll drop the plant on his own accord. Be sure no toxic plants are growing in your own yard or kept in your home. Ask your vet for information on poisonous plants or research them at your library.

The dam instinctively knows when it's time to say "goodbye" to her unruly demanding brood.

crate or on a friend's warm lap. He's been to the vet for a thorough check-up, he's been weighed, his papers examined; perhaps he's even been vaccinated and wormed as well. He's met the family, licked the whole family, including the excited children and the less-than-happy cat. He's explored his area, his new bed, the yard and anywhere else he's been permitted. He's eaten his first meal at home and relieved himself in the proper place. He's heard lots of new sounds, smelled new friends and seen more of the outside world than ever before.

That was just the first day! He's worn out and is ready for bed...or so you think!

It's puppy's first night and you are ready to say "Good night"— keep in mind that this is puppy's first night ever to be sleeping

himself with exploring for a while. Gradually, each person should spend some time with the pup, one at a time, crouching down to get as close to the pup's level as possible and letting him sniff their hands and petting him gently. He definitely needs human attention and he needs to be touched—this is how to form an immediate bond. Just remember that the pup is experiencing a lot of things for the first time, at the same time. There are new people, new noises, new smells and new things to investigate: so be gentle, be affectionate and be as comforting as you can be.

YOUR PUP'S FIRST NIGHT HOME

You have traveled home with your new charge safely in his

THE RIDE HOME

Taking your dog from the breeder to your home in a car can be a very uncomfortable experience for both of you. The puppy will have been taken from his warm, friendly, safe environment and brought into a strange new environment—an environment that moves! Be prepared for loose bowels, urination, crying, whining and even fear biting. With proper love and encouragement when you arrive home, the stress of the trip should quickly disappear.

alone. His dam and littermates are no longer at paw's length and he's a bit scared, cold and lonely. Be reassuring to your new family member. This is not the time to spoil him and give in to his inevitable whining.

Puppies whine. They whine to let the others know where they are and hopefully to get company out of it. Place your pup in his new bed or crate in his room and close the door. Mercifully, he may fall asleep without a peep. When the inevitable occurs, ignore the whining: he is fine. Be strong and keep his interest in mind. Do not allow your heart to become guilty and visit the pup. He will fall asleep.

Many breeders recommend placing a piece of bedding from his former home in his new bed so that he recognizes the scent of his littermates. Others still advise placing a hot water bottle in his bed for warmth. This latter may be a good idea provided the pup doesn't attempt to suckle—he'll get good and wet and may not fall asleep so fast.

Puppy's first night can be somewhat stressful for the pup and his new family. Remember that you are setting the tone of nighttime at your house. Unless you want to play with your pup every evening at 10 p.m., midnight and 2 a.m., don't initiate the habit. Your family will thank you, and so will your pup!

PREVENTING PUPPY PROBLEMS

SOCIALIZATION
Now that you have done all of the preparatory work and have helped your pup get accustomed to his new home and family, it is about

When a child and a Cairn grow up together, there is an unmistakable bond that develops between them.

FEEDING TIPS
You will probably start feeding your pup the same food that he has been getting from the breeder; the breeder should give you a few days' supply to start you off. Although you should not give your pup too many treats, you will want to have puppy treats on hand for coaxing, training, rewards, etc. Be careful, though, as a small pup's calorie requirements are relatively low and a few treats can add up to almost a full day's worth of calories without the required nutrition.

Cairns are friendly, intelligent dogs. Some of their best friends can be cats! It all depends upon a process called socialization.

time for you to have some fun! Socializing your Cairn Terrier pup gives you the opportunity to show off your new friend, and your pup gets to reap the benefits of being an adorable furry creature that people will want to pet and, in general, think is absolutely precious!

PUP MEETS WORLD

Thorough socialization includes not only meeting new people but also being introduced to new experiences such as riding in the car, having his coat brushed, hearing the television, walking in a crowd—the list is endless. The more your pup experiences, and the more positive the experiences are, the less of a shock and the less frightening it will be for your pup to encounter new things.

Besides getting to know his new family, your puppy should be exposed to other people, animals and situations, but of course he must not come into close contact with dogs you don't know well until his course of injections is fully complete. This will help him become well adjusted as he grows up and less prone to being timid or fearful of the new things he will encounter. Your pup's socialization began at the breeder's but now it is your responsibility to continue it. The socialization he receives up until the age of 12 weeks is the most critical, as this is the time when he forms his impressions of the outside world. Be especially careful during the eight-to-ten-week period, also known as the fear period. The interaction he receives during this time should be gentle and reassuring. Lack of socialization can manifest itself in fear and aggression as the dog grows up. He needs lots of human contact, affection, handling and exposure to other animals.

Once your pup has received his necessary vaccinations, feel free to take him out and about (on his lead, of course). Walk him around the neighborhood, take him on your daily errands, let people pet him, let him meet other dogs and pets, etc. Puppies do not have to try to make friends; there will be no shortage of people who will want to

Socialized, happy dogs get along photogenically with each other as well as the people they meet.

When you first bring your Cairn puppy home, he only has the imprint of family life with his own mother. You are responsible for teaching your Cairn how to exist in the human world.

introduce themselves. Just make sure that you carefully supervise each meeting. If the neighborhood children want to say hello, for example, that is great—children and pups most often make great companions. Sometimes an excited child can unintentionally handle a pup too roughly, or an overzealous pup can playfully nip a little too hard. You want to make socialization experiences positive ones. What a pup learns during this very formative stage will impact his attitude toward future encounters. You want your dog to be comfortable around everyone. A pup that has a bad experience with a child may grow up to be a dog that is shy around or aggressive toward children.

CONSISTENCY IN TRAINING

Dogs, being pack animals, naturally need a leader, or else they try to establish dominance in their packs. When you bring a dog

into your family, the choice of who becomes the leader and who becomes the "pack" is entirely up to you! Your pup's intuitive quest for dominance, coupled with the fact that it is nearly impossible to look at an adorable Cairn Terrier pup, with his "puppy-dog" eyes and his wiry face, and not cave in, give the pup almost an unfair advantage in getting the upper hand! A pup will definitely test the waters to see what he can and cannot do. Do not give in to those pleading eyes—stand your ground when it comes to disciplining the pup and make sure that all family members do the same. It will only confuse the pup when Mother tells him to get off the couch when he is used to sitting up there with Father to watch the nightly news. Avoid discrepancies

Cairns, like other terriers, are dog-aggressive. If properly socialized with other dogs, your Cairn will accept other dogs when introduced on neutral ground.

> **TRAINING TIP**
>
> Training your puppy takes much patience and can be frustrating at times, but you should see results from your efforts. If you have a puppy that seems untrainable, take him to a trainer or behaviorist. The dog may have a personality problem that requires the help of a professional, or perhaps you need help in learning how to train your dog.

Cairns have minds of their own. Make your impression on your pup before he's a headstrong teenager.

by having all members of the household decide on the rules before the pup even comes home…and be consistent in enforcing them! Early training shapes the dog's personality, so you cannot be unclear in what you expect.

COMMON PUPPY PROBLEMS

The best way to prevent puppy problems is to be proactive in stopping an undesirable behavior as soon as it starts. The old saying "You can't teach an old dog new

All dogs learn by watching, and your pup learned most of his lessons from his dam. Are you ready to assume the role of master and teacher?

tricks" does not necessarily hold true, but it is true that it is much easier to discourage bad behavior in a young developing pup than to wait until the pup's bad behavior becomes the adult dog's bad habit. There are some problems that are especially prevalent in puppies as they develop.

NIPPING

As puppies start to teethe, they feel the need to sink their teeth into anything available...unfortunately that includes your fingers, arms, hair and toes. You may find this behavior cute for the first five seconds...until you feel just how sharp those puppy teeth are. This is something you want to discourage immediately and consistently with a firm "No!" (or whatever number of firm "Nos" it takes for him to understand that you mean business). Then replace your finger with an appropriate chew toy. While this behavior is merely annoying when the dog is young, it can become dangerous as your Cairn Terrier's adult teeth grow in and his jaws develop, and he continues to think it is okay to gnaw on human appendages. Your Cairn Terrier does not mean any harm with a friendly nip, but even a small dog can have a big bite if he doesn't know any better.

CRYING/WHINING

Your pup will often cry, whine, whimper, howl or make some

> ## CHEWING TIPS
> Chewing goes hand in hand with nipping in the sense that a teething puppy is always looking for a way to soothe his aching gums. In this case, instead of chewing on you, he may have taken a liking to your favorite shoe or something else that he should not be chewing. Again, realize that this is a normal canine behavior that does not need to be discouraged, only redirected. Your pup just needs to be taught what is acceptable to chew on and what is off-limits. Consistently tell him "No!" when you catch him chewing on something forbidden and give him a chew toy.
>
> Conversely, praise him when you catch him chewing on something appropriate. In this way, you are discouraging the inappropriate behavior and reinforcing the desired behavior. The puppy's chewing should stop after his adult teeth have come in, but an adult dog continues to chew for various reasons—perhaps because he is bored, needs to relieve tension or just likes to chew. That is why it is important to redirect his chewing when he is still young.

type of commotion when he is left alone. This is basically his way of calling out for attention to make sure that you know he is there and that you have not forgotten about him. He feels insecure when he is left alone, when you are out of the house and he is in

The first time you put a collar on your Cairn puppy, it might very well upset him and he will attempt to scratch it off.

his crate or when you are in another part of the house and he cannot see you. The noise he is making is an expression of the anxiety he feels at being alone, so he needs to be taught that being alone is okay. You are not actually training the dog to stop making noise, you are training him to feel comfortable when he is alone and thus removing the need for him to make the noise. This is where the crate with cozy bedding and a toy comes in handy. You want to know that he is safe when you are not there to supervise, and you know that he will be safe in his crate rather than roaming freely about the house. In order for the pup to stay in his crate without making a fuss, he needs to be comfortable in his crate. On that note, it is extremely important that the crate is never used as a form of punishment, or the pup will have a negative association with the crate.

The majority of problems that are commonly seen in young pups will disappear as your dog gets older. However, how you deal with problems when he is young

Many Cairns love the water, and are excellent swimmers, but they should not be allowed access to the water without proper supervision.

STRESS-FREE

Some experts in canine health advise that stress during a dog's early years of development can compromise and weaken his immune system, and may trigger the potential for a shortened life. They emphasize the need for happy and stress-free growing-up years.

PUPPY PROBLEMS

The majority of problems that are commonly seen in young pups will disappear as your dog gets older. However, how you deal with problems when he is young will determine how he reacts to discipline as an adult dog. It is important to establish who is boss (ideally it will be you!) right away when you are first bonding with your dog. This bond will set the tone for the rest of your life together.

will determine how he reacts to discipline as an adult dog. It is important to establish who is boss (hopefully it will be you!) right away when you are first bonding with your dog. This bond will set the tone for the rest of your life

together. Accustom the pup to the crate in short, gradually increasing time intervals in which you put him in the crate, maybe with a treat, and stay in the room with him. If he cries or makes a fuss, do not go to him, but stay in his sight. Gradually he will realize that staying in his crate is just fine without your help, and it will not be so traumatic for him when you are not around. You may want to leave the radio on softly when you leave the house; the sound of human voices may be comforting to him.

Your Cairn will accept his crate as a safe haven and not feel lonely when he is placed in it.

DIETARY AND FEEDING CONSIDERATIONS

Today the choices of food for your Cairn Terrier are many and varied. There are simply dozens of brands of food in all sorts of flavors and textures, ranging from puppy diets to those for seniors. There are even hypoallergenic and low-calorie diets available. Because your Cairn Terrier's food has a bearing on coat, health and temperament, it is essential that the most suitable diet is selected for a Cairn Terrier of his age. It is fair to say, however, that even dedicated owners can be somewhat perplexed by the enormous range of foods available. Only understanding what is best for your dog will help you reach an informed decision.

Dog foods are produced in three basic types: dry, semi-moist and canned. Dry foods are useful for the cost-conscious for overall they tend to be less expensive than semi-moist or canned. These contain the least fat and the most preservatives. In general, canned foods are made up of 60–70% water, while semi-moist ones often contain so much sugar that they are perhaps the least

preferred by owners, even though their dogs seem to like them. When selecting your dog's diet, three stages of development must be considered: the puppy stage, the adult stage and the senior stage.

PUPPY STAGE

Puppies instinctively want to suck milk from their mother's teats and a normal puppy will exhibit this behavior from just a few moments following birth. If puppies do not attempt to suckle within the first half-hour or so, the breeder must place them on the nipples, having selected ones with plenty of milk. This early milk supply is important in providing colostrum to protect the puppies during the first eight to ten weeks of their lives. Although a mother's milk is

TEST FOR PROPER DIET

A good test for proper diet is the color, odor and firmness of your dog's stool. A healthy dog usually produces three semi-hard stools per day. The stools should have no unpleasant odor. They should be the same color from excretion to excretion.

Puppies always seem to be hungry. They require a special diet while) they are still in their fast-growing period.

FOOD PREFERENCE

Selecting the best dry dog food is difficult. There is no majority consensus among veterinary scientists as to the value of nutrient analysis (protein, fat, fiber, moisture, ash, cholesterol, minerals, etc.). All agree that feeding trials are what matter most, but you also have to consider the individual dog. The dog's weight, age and activity level, and what pleases his taste, all must be considered. It is probably best to take the advice of your veterinarian. Every dog has individual dietary requirements, and should be fed accordingly.

If your dog is fed a good dry food, he does not require supplements of meat or vegetables. Dogs do appreciate a little variety in their diets, so you may choose to stay with the same brand but vary the flavor. Alternatively, you may wish to add a little flavored stock to give a difference to the taste.

much better than any milk formula, despite there being some excellent ones available, if the puppies do not feed, the breeder has to feed them himself. For those with less experience, advice from a veterinarian is important so that not only the right quantity of milk is offered but that of correct quality, fed at suitably frequent intervals, usually every two hours during the first few days of life.

Puppies should be allowed to nurse from their mother for about the first six weeks, although from the third or fourth week you will have begun to introduce small portions of suitable solid food. Most breeders like to introduce alternate milk and meat meals initially, building up to weaning time.

By the time the puppies are seven or a maximum of eight weeks old, they should be fully weaned and fed solely on a

Puppy and junior diets should be well balanced for the needs of your dog, so that except in certain circumstances additional vitamins, minerals and proteins will not be required.

ADULT DIETS

A dog is considered an adult when he has stopped growing, so in general the diet of a Cairn Terrier can be changed to an adult one at about 12 months of age. Again you should rely upon your veterinarian or breeder to recommend an acceptable maintenance diet. Major dog food manufacturers specialize in this type of food, and it is just necessary for you to select the one

Cairn puppies should be allowed to nurse for the first six weeks of their lives. By the time your Cairn is ready to come home, he will be completely weaned.

proprietary puppy food. Selection of the most suitable, good-quality diet at this time is essential for a puppy's fastest growth rate is during the first year of life. Veterinarians are usually able to offer advice in this regard and, although the frequency of meals will have been reduced over time, only when a young dog has reached the age of about 12 months should an adult diet be fed.

best suited to your dog's needs. Active dogs may have different requirements than sedentary dogs.

SENIOR DIETS

As dogs get older, their metabolism changes. The older dog usually exercises less, moves more slowly and sleeps more. This change in lifestyle and physiological performance requires a change in diet. Since these changes take place slowly, they might not be recognizable. What is easily recognizable is weight gain. By continuing to feed your dog an adult-maintenance diet when he is slowing down metabolically, your dog will gain weight. Obesity in an older dog

GRAIN-BASED DIETS

Some less expensive dog foods are based on grains and other plant proteins. While these products may appear to be attractively priced, many breeders prefer a diet based on animal proteins and believe that they are more conducive to your dog's health. Many grain-based diets rely on soy protein, which may cause flatulence (passing gas).

There are many cases, however, when your dog might require a special diet. These special requirements should only be recommended by your veterinarian.

compounds the health problems that already accompany old age.

As dogs get older, few of their organs function up to par. The kidneys slow down and the intestines become less efficient. These age-related factors are best handled with a change in diet and a change in feeding schedule to give smaller portions that are more easily digested.

There is no single best diet for every older dog. While many dogs do well on light or senior diets, other dogs do better on puppy diets or other special premium diets such as lamb and rice. Be sensitive to your senior Cairn Terrier's diet and this will help control other problems that may arise with your old friend.

Competition around the feeding pan enhances the appetites of young pups. Once the pup is brought into your home, he may "wolf" his food voraciously. In time, he'll eat at a more leisurely pace.

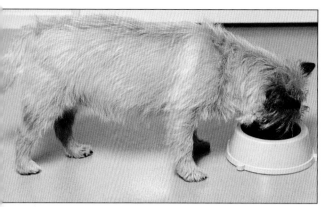

WATER

Water must always be available for adults, unless there are medical reasons to withhold the water. During the housebreaking process, a pup's water intake must be monitored.

Just as your dog needs proper nutrition from his food, water is an essential "nutrient" as well. Water keeps the dog's body properly hydrated and promotes normal function of the body's systems. During housebreaking it is necessary to keep an eye on how much water your Cairn Terrier is drinking, but once he is reliably trained he should have access to clean fresh water at all times. Make sure that the dog's water bowl is clean, and change the water often, making sure that water is always available for your dog, especially if you feed dry food.

EXERCISE

Although a Cairn Terrier is small, all dogs require some form of exercise, regardless of breed. A sedentary lifestyle is as harmful to a dog as it is to a person. The Cairn Terrier is a fairly active breed that enjoys exercise, but you don't have to be an Olympic athlete! Regular walks, play sessions in the yard, or letting the dog run free in the yard under your supervision are sufficient forms of exercise for the Cairn Terrier. For those who are more ambitious, you will find that your Cairn Terrier also enjoys long walks, an occasional hike or even a swim! Bear in mind that an overweight dog should never be over-exercised; instead he should be allowed to increase exercise slowly. Not only is exercise essential to keep the dog's body fit, it is essential to his mental well-being. A bored dog will find something to do, which often manifests itself in some type of destructive behavior. In this sense, it is essential for the owner's mental well-being as well!

GROOMING

Whether you have chosen the Cairn Terrier as a show dog or simply as a companion around your home, he will require a certain amount of grooming to look presentable and tidy. Although the Cairn's coat is not the most difficult coat in the Terrier Group to maintain, it does present demands on the owner. Remember, you cannot take a Cairn to a groomer and tell him to shave him down as you can a Poodle. This is a much different coat.

The Cairn is a double-coated

A Worthy Investment

**Veterinary studies have proven that a balanced high-quality diet
pays off in your dog's coat quality, behavior and activity level.
Invest in premium brands for the maximum payoff with your dog.**

Your local pet shop has a wide supply of dog brushes from which you may select the ones that suit your needs.

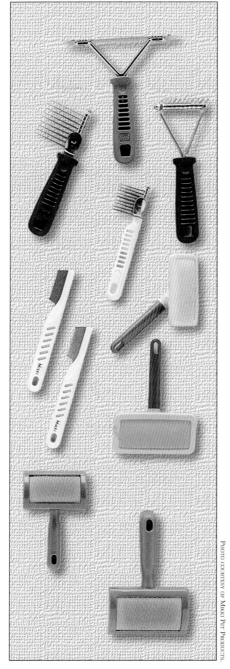

dog. There is a dense, thick undercoat that protects the dog in all kinds of weather and there is a harsh outercoat. Coat care for the pet Cairn can be much less time-consuming and easier than the coat care for a show dog. The vast majority of Cairn fanciers has a dog for a pet and should not expect to maintain a show coat.

If you are planning to show your Cairn Terrier, you are well advised to discuss the grooming and conditioning with the breeder from whom you acquired your puppy. Most reputable breeders groom and show their own dogs. Visit the breeder with your puppy for grooming lessons to learn how to get your dog ready for the show

GROOMING EQUIPMENT

Always purchase the best quality grooming equipment so that your tools will last for many years to come. Here are some basics:

- Slicker brush
- Metal comb
- Scissors
- Grooming table with mat and arm
- Dog shampoo
- Spray hose attachment
- Towels
- Blow dryer
- Ear cleaner
- Cotton balls
- Nail clippers
- Dental care products

ring. Grooming for the show is an art, and an art that cannot be learned in a few months. The primary difference between the pet and show Cairn coat is that the show Cairn will have a dense undercoat and on top of it he will have a tidy, harsh coat. With the proper coat, the dog presents a smartness in the ring that can be hard to beat. This coat can only be acquired by stripping the body coat, twice a year, with a stripping knife or stripping by hand. This all takes skill, time and interest in order to do it well. Pet grooming is different than grooming for the show ring and you will not have the harsh, tidy coat of the show Cairn, but you will have a neat, clean and trimmed dog that will still look like a Cairn Terrier.

In order to groom your Cairn Terrier, you will need:

1. A grooming table, something sturdy with a rubber mat covering the top. You will need a grooming arm, or a "hanger." (You can use a table in your laundry room with an eye hook in the ceiling for holding the leash.) Your dog will now be comfortable even if confined and you will be able to work on the dog. Grooming is a very difficult and frustrating job if you try to groom without a table and a grooming arm.
2. A metal comb, a slicker brush, a good sharp pair of scissors and a toenail trimmer.

Getting ready for show presentation. A sturdy grooming table, adjustable to suit your height, is necessary to allow you to groom your Cairn comfortably.

To start, set your dog on the table and put the leash around his neck. Have your leash up behind the ears and have the leash taut when you fasten it to your eye hook. Do not walk away and leave your dog unattended as he can jump off the table and be left dangling from the leash with his feet scrambling around in the air.

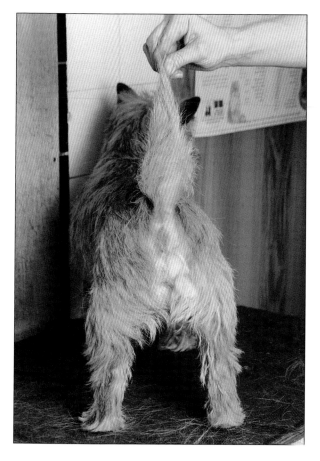

The Cairn's tail looks unkempt before the loose hairs are plucked.

trim the area around the penis. With the girls, trim some of the hair around the vulva.

Now that your dog is brushed out, comb through the coat with your metal comb. By now you have removed a fair amount of dead hair and your dog will already be looking better. You may find some small mats and these can be worked out with your fingers or your comb. If you brush your dog out every week or so, you will not have too much of a problem with the mats.

When you find that the coat is separating, you should be prepared to do some hand-stripping, which means pulling out the dead, long coat, in the direction in which it lies. It is best to have a stripping knife for this process and it is helpful if your breeder or someone else can show you how this is to be done. Of course, you can clip your dog down, leaving a trimmed head, and within eight to ten weeks, your dog will have a soft, but nice coat.

If this is your first experience, you may be a bit clumsy, but the hair will grow back in a short time. The finished product may not be quite what you had expected, but expertise will come with experience and you will soon be very proud of your efforts. Put your dog in the bathtub when you are finished and give him a good bath and rinsing. After

Take your slicker brush and brush out the entire coat. Brush the whiskers toward the nose, the body hair toward the tail, the tail up toward its tip. Brush the leg furnishings up toward the body and brush the chest hair down toward the table. Hold the dog up by the front legs and gently brush the stomach hair, first toward the head and then back toward the rear. For cleanliness, you may want to take your scissors and

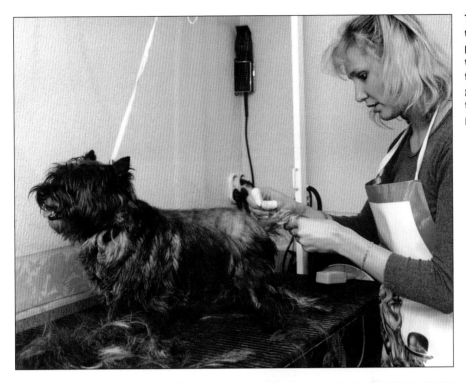

This Cairn is being trimmed and plucked. Notice the rubber fingertips on the groomer. These facilitate plucking.

toweling him down, return him to the grooming table and trim the toenails on all four feet. At this point you can dry your dog with a blow dryer and brush him out again. Or, you can let him dry naturally and then brush him out. If you have grooming problems, you can take your dog to the professional groomer the first time or two for his grooming. (Of course, you can eliminate all of the grooming for yourself, except for the weekly brushing, if you take your dog to the groomer every three months!) Just remember, many pet owners can do a much better job trimming

Your Cairn may never truly appreciate the grooming process, but he will learn to accept it. This type of training starts at an early age. For such small terriers, they certainly cast an abundant coat.

SOAP IT UP

The use of human soap products like shampoo, bubble bath and hand soap can be damaging to a dog's coat and skin. Human products are too strong; they remove the protective oils coating the dog's hair and skin that make him water-resistant. Use only shampoo made especially for dogs. You may like to use a medicated shampoo, which will help to keep external parasites at bay.

their dogs than some so-called professional groomers.

In general, your pet should be brushed weekly and bathed as needed. Trim the toenails every month or so and plan to clip the dog every three months. Follow this plan and your dog will be clean, he will have a new "dress" every three months, and he will look like a Cairn Terrier!

BATHING

Dogs do not need to be bathed as often as humans, but regular bathing is essential for healthy skin and a clean, shiny coat. Again, like most anything, if you accustom your pup to being bathed as a puppy, it will be second nature by the time he grows up. You want your dog to be at ease in the bath or else it could end up a wet, soapy, messy ordeal for both of you!

Brush your Cairn Terrier thoroughly before wetting his coat. This will get rid of most mats and tangles, which are harder to remove when the coat is wet. Make sure that your dog has a good non-slip surface to stand on. Begin by wetting the dog's coat. A shower or hose attachment is necessary for thoroughly wetting and rinsing the coat. Check the water temperature to make sure that it is neither too hot nor too cold.

Next, apply shampoo to the dog's coat and work it into a good lather. You should purchase a shampoo that is made for dogs. Do not use a product made for human hair. Wash the head last; you do not want shampoo to drip into the dog's eyes while you are washing the rest of his body. Work the shampoo all the way down to the skin. You can use this opportunity to check the skin for any bumps, bites or other abnormalities. Do not neglect any area of the body— get all of the hard-to-reach places.

Once the dog has been thoroughly shampooed, he requires an equally thorough rinsing. Shampoo left in the coat can be irritating to the skin. Protect his eyes from the shampoo by shielding them with your hand and directing the flow of water in the opposite direction. You should also avoid getting water in the ear canal. Be prepared for your dog to shake out his coat—

you might want to stand back, but make sure you have a hold on the dog to keep him from running through the house.

EAR CLEANING

The ears should be kept clean and any excess hair inside the ear should be carefully plucked out. Ears can be cleaned with cotton balls and an ear-cleaning solution made especially for dogs. Be on the lookout for any signs of infection or ear-mite infestation. If your Cairn Terrier has been shaking his head or scratching at his ears frequently, this usually indicates a problem. If his ears have an unusual odor, this is a sure sign of mite infestation or

BATHING BEAUTY

Once you are sure that the dog is thoroughly rinsed, squeeze the excess water out of his coat with your hand and dry him with an heavy towel. You may choose to use a blow dryer on his coat or just let it dry naturally. In cold weather, never allow your dog outside with a wet coat.

There are "dry bath" products on the market, which are sprays and powders intended for spot cleaning, that can be used between regular baths if necessary. They are not substitutes for regular baths, but they are easy to use for touch-ups as they do not require rinsing.

bleed if accidentally cut, which will be quite painful for the dog as it contains nerve endings. Keep some type of clotting agent on hand, such as a styptic pencil or styptic powder (the type used for shaving). This will stop the bleeding quickly when applied to the end of the cut nail. Do not panic if this happens, just stop the bleeding and talk soothingly to your dog. Once he has calmed down, move on to the next nail. It is better to clip a little at a time, particularly with black-nailed dogs.

Hold your pup steady as you begin trimming his nails; you do not want him to make any sudden movements or run away. Talk to him soothingly and stroke him as you clip. Holding his foot in your hand, simply take off the end of each nail in one quick clip. You can purchase nail clippers that are

A blow dryer should be used to dry the Cairn's coat thoroughly. Be careful that the air is not too hot for the dog's delicate skin.

The ears should be cleaned regularly. Be alert to ear mites or any debris that might be visible while you are cleaning the ear.

infection, and a signal to have his ears checked by the veterinarian.

NAIL CLIPPING

Your Cairn Terrier should be accustomed to having his nails trimmed at an early age, since it will be a part of your maintenance routine throughout his life. Not only does it look nicer, but long, sharp nails can scratch someone unintentionally. Also, a long nail has a better chance of ripping and bleeding, or causing the feet to spread. A good rule of thumb is that if you can hear your dog's nails clicking on the floor when he walks, his nails are too long.

Before you start cutting, make sure you can identify the "quick" in each nail. The quick is a blood vessel that runs through the center of each nail and grows rather close to the end. It will

Nail Clipping

Quick

Cut Line **Nail Casing**

DARK-COLORED NAIL

With black or dark nails, it's best to clip only a small bit of the nail at a time or to use a file where the quick is not visible.

LIGHT-COLORED NAIL

In light-colored nails, clipping is much simpler because you can see the vein (or quick) that grows inside the casing.

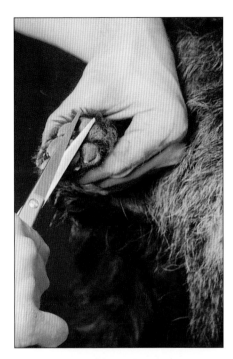

The hair on the bottom of the foot must be trimmed carefully.

The guillotine-style nail clippers will work most effectively on your Cairn's toenails.

Your Cairn Terrier should never be allowed complete freedom in your car while you are driving.

specially made for dogs; you can probably find them wherever you buy pet or grooming supplies.

TRAVELING WITH YOUR DOG

CAR TRAVEL

You should accustom your Cairn Terrier to riding in a car at an early age. You may or may not take him in the car often, but at the very least he will need to go to the vet and you do not want these trips to be traumatic for the dog or a big hassle for you. The safest way for a dog to ride in the car is in his crate. If he uses a crate in the house, you can use the same crate for travel.

Put the pup in the crate and see how he reacts. If he seems uneasy, you can have a passenger hold him on his lap while you drive. Another option is a specially made safety harness for dogs, which straps the dog in much like a seat belt. Do not let the dog roam loose in the vehicle—this is very dangerous! If you should stop short, your dog can be thrown and injured. If the dog starts climbing on you and pestering you while you are driving, you will not be able to concentrate on the road. It is an unsafe situation for everyone— human and canine.

For long trips, be prepared to stop to let the dog relieve himself. Bring along whatever you need to clean up after him. You should take along some paper towels and perhaps some old rags for use should he have an accident in the car or suffer from motion sickness.

AIR TRAVEL

Contact your chosen airline before proceeding with your travel plans that include your Cairn Terrier. The dog will be required to travel in a fiberglass crate and you should always check in advance with the airline regarding specific requirements for the crate's size, type and labeling. To help put the

TOO HOT TO HANDLE

Never leave your dog alone in the car. In hot weather, your dog can die from the high temperature inside a closed vehicle; even a car parked in the shade can heat up very quickly. Leaving the window open is dangerous as well since the dog can hurt himself trying to get out.

dog at ease, give him one of his favorite toys in the crate. Do not feed the dog for several hours prior to checking in so that you minimize his need to relieve himself. However, some airlines require that the dog must be fed within four hours of arriving at the airport, in which case a light meal is best. For long trips, you will have to attach food and water bowls to the dog's crate so that airline employees can tend to him between legs of the trip.

VACATION AND BOARDING

So you want to take a family vacation—and you want to include all members of the family. You would probably make arrangements for accommodations ahead of time anyway, but this is especially important when traveling with a dog. You do not want to make an overnight stop at the only place around for miles and find out that they do not allow dogs. Also, you do not want to reserve a place for your family without confirming that you are traveling with a dog because if it is against their policy you may not have a place to stay.

Alternatively, if you are traveling and choose not to bring your Cairn Terrier, you will have to make arrangements for him while you are away. Some options are to take him to a neighbor's house to stay while you are gone, to have a trusted neighbor stop by

> **TRAVEL TIP**
> When traveling, never let your dog off-lead in a strange area. Your dog could run away out of fear, decide to chase a passing squirrel or cat or simply want to stretch his legs without restriction—if any of these happen, you might never see your canine friend again.

often or stay at your house, or bring your dog to a reputable boarding kennel.

If you choose to board him at a kennel, you should visit in advance to see the facilities provided, how clean they are and where the dogs are kept. Talk to some of the employees and see how they treat the dogs—do they spend time with the dogs, play with them, exercise them, etc.? Also find out the kennel's policy on vaccinations and what they require. This is for all of the dogs' safety, since when dogs are kept

The Cairn is a small enough dog to be able to comfortably be restrained in a crate in your car.

TRAVELING ABROAD

For international travel you will have to make arrangements well in advance (perhaps months), as countries' regulations pertaining to bringing in animals differ. There may be special health certificates and/or vaccinations that your dog will need before taking the trip; sometimes this has to be done within a certain time frame. In rabies-free countries, you will need to bring proof of the dog's rabies vaccination and there may be a quarantine period upon arrival.

Have a suitable boarding kennel in mind before you actually need to use it. Check for cleanliness, size and convenience of location, as well as a professional staff and services provided, such as grooming.

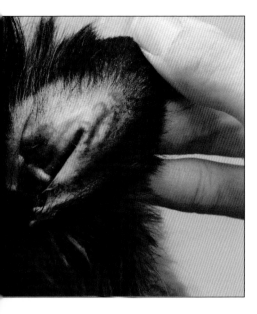

together, there is a risk of diseases being passed from dog to dog.

IDENTIFICATION

Your Cairn Terrier is your valued companion and friend. That is why you always keep a close eye on him and you have made sure that he cannot escape from the yard or wriggle out of his collar and run away from you. However, accidents can happen and there may come a time when your dog unexpectedly gets separated from you. If this unfortunate event should occur, the first thing on your mind will be finding him. Proper identification, including an ID tag, a tattoo and possibly a microchip, will increase the chances of his being returned to you safely and quickly.

IDENTIFICATION OPTIONS

As puppies become more and more expensive, especially those puppies of high quality for showing and/or breeding, they have a greater chance of being stolen. The usual collar dog tag is, of course, easily removed. But there are two more permanent techniques that have become widely used for identification.

The puppy microchip implantation involves the injection of a small microchip, about the size of a corn kernel, under the skin of the dog. If your dog shows up at a clinic or shelter, or is offered for resale under less-than-savory circumstances, it can be positively identified by the microchip. The microchip is scanned, and a registry quickly identifies you as the owner.

Tattooing is done on various parts of the dog, from his belly to his ears. The number tattooed can be your telephone number, your dog's registration number or any other number that you can easily memorize. When professional dog thieves see a tattooed dog, they usually lose interest. For the safety of our dogs, no laboratory facility or dog broker will accept a tattooed dog as stock.

Discuss microchipping and tattooing with your veterinarian and breeder. Some vets perform these services on their own premises for a reasonable fee. To ensure that your dog's identification is effective, be certain that the dog is then properly registered with a legitimate national database.

Many valuable Cairns are tattooed underneath their ears (or inside their thighs) so they can be identified if lost or stolen.

TRAINING YOUR
CAIRN TERRIER

Begin your Cairn puppy's home education *before* he starts producing those distracting hormones.

Living with an untrained dog is a lot like owning a piano that you do not know how to play—it is a nice object to look at but it does not do much more than that to bring you pleasure. Now try taking piano lessons and suddenly the piano comes alive and brings forth magical sounds and rhythms that set your heart singing and your body swaying.

The same is true with your Cairn Terrier. Any dog is a big responsibility and if not trained sensibly may develop unacceptable behavior that annoys you or could even cause family friction.

To train your Cairn Terrier, you may like to enroll in an obedience class. Teach him good manners as you learn how and why he behaves the way he does. Find out how to communicate with your dog and how to recognize and understand his communications with you. Suddenly the dog takes on a new role in your life—he is clever, interesting, well behaved and fun to be with. He demonstrates his bond of devotion to you daily. In other words, your Cairn Terrier does wonders for your ego because he constantly reminds you that you are not only his leader, you are his hero!

OBEDIENCE SCHOOL

Taking your dog to an obedience school may be the best investment in time and money you can ever make. You will enjoy the benefits for the lifetime of your dog and you will have the opportunity to meet people who have similar expectations for companion dogs.

MOUTHING OFF

To a dog's way of thinking, your hands are like his mouth in terms of a defense mechanism. If you squeeze him too tightly, he might just bite you because that would be his normal response. This is not aggressive biting and, although all biting should be discouraged, you need the discipline in learning how to handle your dog.

Those involved with teaching dog obedience and counseling owners about their dogs' behavior have discovered some interesting facts about dog ownership. For example, training dogs when they are puppies results in the highest rate of success in developing well-mannered and well-adjusted adult dogs. Training an older dog, from six months to six years of age, can produce almost equal results providing that the owner accepts the dog's slower rate of learning capability and is willing to work patiently to help the dog succeed at developing to his fullest potential. Unfortunately, many owners of untrained adult dogs lack the patience factor, so they do not persist until their dogs are successful at learning particular behaviors.

Training a puppy aged 10 to 16 weeks (20 weeks at the most) is like working with a dry sponge in a pool of water. The pup soaks up whatever you show him and constantly looks for more things to do and learn. At this early age, his body is not yet producing hormones, and therein lies the reason for such a high rate of success. Without hormones, he is focused on his owners and not particularly interested in investigating other places, dogs, people, etc. You are his leader: his provider of food, water, shelter and security. He latches onto you and wants to stay close. He will usually follow you from room to room,

An eight-week-old Cairn puppy with a collar and lead attached for the first time. Lead training and housebreaking go hand and hand.

Nothing gets a
Cairn's attention
better than a
tasty treat!

will not let you out of his sight
when you are outdoors with
him, and respond in like manner
to the people and animals you
encounter. If you greet a friend
warmly, he will be happy to
greet the person as well. If,
however, you are hesitant, even
anxious, about the approach of a

stranger, he will respond accordingly.

Once the puppy begins to
produce hormones, his natural
curiosity emerges and he begins
to investigate the world around
him. It is at this time when you
may notice that the untrained
dog begins to wander away from
you and even ignore your
commands to stay close. When
this behavior becomes a
problem, the owner has two
choices: get rid of the dog or
train him. It is strongly urged
that you choose the latter
option.

There are usually classes
within a reasonable distance
from the owner's home, but you
also do a lot to train your dog

THINK BEFORE YOU BARK
Dogs are sensitive to their masters'
moods and emotions. Use your
voice wisely when communicating
with your dog. Never raise your
voice at your dog unless you are
trying to correct him. "Barking" at
your dog can become as meaning-
less as "dogspeak" is to you.

yourself. Sometimes there are classes available but the tuition is too costly. Whatever the circumstances, the solution to training your Cairn Terrier at home without a professional instructor lies within the pages of this book. This chapter is devoted to helping you train your Cairn Terrier at home. If the recommended procedures are followed faithfully, you may expect positive results that will prove rewarding to both you and your dog.

Whether your new charge is a puppy or a mature adult, the methods of teaching and the techniques we use in training basic behaviors are the same. After all, no dog, whether puppy or adult, likes harsh or inhumane methods. All creatures, however, respond favorably to gentle motivational methods and sincere praise and encouragement. Now let us get started.

HOUSEBREAKING

You can train a puppy to relieve himself wherever you choose, but this must be somewhere suitable. You should bear in mind from the outset that when your puppy is old enough to go out in public places, any canine droppings must be removed at once. You will always have to carry with you a small plastic bag or "poop-scoop."

Outdoor training includes such surfaces as grass, soil and cement. Indoor training usually means training your dog to newspaper.

When deciding on the surface and location that you will want your Cairn Terrier to

You must train your Cairn to relieve himself when and where you want. All droppings should be cleaned up whether in a public place or your own yard.

THE CLEAN LIFE
By providing sleeping and resting quarters that fit the dog, and offering frequent opportunities to relieve himself outside his quarters, the puppy quickly learns that the outdoors (or the newspaper if you are training him to paper) is the place to go when he needs to urinate or defecate. It also reinforces his innate desire to keep his sleeping quarters clean. This, in turn, helps develop the muscle control that will eventually produce a dog with clean living habits.

use, be sure it is going to be permanent. Training your dog to grass and then changing your mind two months later is extremely difficult for both dog and owner.

Next, choose the command you will use each and every time you want your puppy to void. "Hurry up" and "Let's go" are examples of commands commonly used by dog owners. Get in the habit of giving the puppy your chosen relief command before you take him out. That way, when he becomes an adult, you will be able to determine if he wants to go out when you ask him. A confirmation will be signs of interest, such as wagging his tail, watching you intently, going to the door and so forth.

PAPER CAPER

Never line your pup's sleeping area with newspaper. Puppy litters are usually raised on newspaper and, once in your home, the puppy will immediately associate newspaper with voiding. Never put newspaper on any floor while house-training, as this will only confuse the puppy. If you are paper-training him, use paper in his designated relief area only. Finally, restrict water intake after evening meals. Offer a few licks at a time— never let a young puppy gulp water after meals.

PUPPY'S NEEDS

Your puppy needs to relieve himself after play periods, after each meal, after he has been sleeping and any time he indicates that he is looking for a place to urinate or defecate. The urinary and intestinal tract muscles of very young puppies are not fully developed. Therefore, like human babies, puppies need to relieve themselves frequently.

Take your puppy out often— every hour for an eight-week-old, for example, and always immediately after sleeping and eating. The older the puppy, the less often he will need to relieve himself. Finally, as a mature healthy adult, he will require only three to five relief trips per day.

HOUSING

Since the type of housing and control you provide for your puppy has a direct relationship on the success of house-training, we consider the various aspects of both before we begin training. Bringing a new puppy home and turning him loose in your house can be compared to turning a child loose in a sports arena and telling the child that the place is all his! The sheer enormity of the place would be too much for him to handle. Instead, offer the puppy clearly defined areas where he can play, sleep, eat and

CANINE DEVELOPMENT SCHEDULE

It is important to understand how and at what age a puppy develops into adulthood. If you are a puppy owner, consult the following Canine Development Schedule to determine the stage of development your puppy is currently experiencing. This knowledge will help you as you work with the puppy in the weeks and months ahead.

Period	Age	Characteristics
First to Third	**Birth to Seven Weeks**	Puppy needs food, sleep and warmth, and responds to simple and gentle touching. Needs mother for security and disciplining. Needs littermates for learning and interacting with other dogs. Pup learns to function within a pack and learns pack order of dominance. Begin socializing pup with adults and children for short periods. Pup begins to become aware of his environment.
Fourth	**Eight to Twelve Weeks**	Brain is fully developed. Pup needs socializing with outside world. Remove from mother and littermates. Needs to change from canine pack to human pack. Human dominance necessary. Fear period occurs between 8 and 12 weeks. Avoid fright and pain.
Fifth	**Thirteen to Sixteen Weeks**	Training and formal obedience should begin. Less association with other dogs, more with people, places, situations. Period will pass easily if you remember this is pup's change-to-adolescence time. Be firm and fair. Flight instinct prominent. Permissiveness and over-disciplining can do permanent damage. Praise for good behavior.
Juvenile	**Four to Eight Months**	Another fear period about 7 to 8 months of age. It passes quickly, but be cautious of fright and pain. Sexual maturity reached. Dominant traits established. Dog should understand sit, down, come and stay by now.

NOTE: THESE ARE APPROXIMATE TIME FRAMES. ALLOW FOR INDIVIDUAL DIFFERENCES IN PUPPIES.

Get your Cairn's lessons off on the right foot! Teach him the dos and don'ts right away.

live. A room of the house where the family gathers is the most obvious choice. Puppies are social animals and need to feel a part of the pack right from the start. Hearing your voice, watching you while you are doing things and smelling you nearby are all positive reinforcers that he is now a member of your pack. Usually a family room, the kitchen or a nearby adjoining breakfast area is ideal for providing safety and security for both puppy and owner.

Within that room there should be a smaller area which the puppy can call his own. An alcove, a wire or fiberglass dog crate or a gated corner from which he can view the activities of his new family will be fine. The size of the area or crate is the key factor here. The area must be large enough for the

TAKE THE LEAD
Do not carry your dog to his relief area. Lead him there on a leash or, better yet, encourage him to follow you to the spot. If you start carrying him to his spot, you might end up doing this routine forever and your dog will have the satisfaction of having trained *you*.

PRACTICE MAKES PERFECT!

- Have training lessons with your dog every day in several short segments—three to five times a day for a few minutes at a time is ideal.
- Do not have long practice sessions. The dog will become easily bored.
- Never practice when you are tired, ill, worried or in an otherwise negative mood. This will transmit to the dog and may have an adverse effect on his performance.

  Think fun, short and above all *positive!* End each session on a high note, rather than a failed exercise, and make sure to give a lot of praise. Enjoy the training and help your dog enjoy it, too.

CONTROL

By *control*, we mean helping the puppy to create a lifestyle pattern that will be compatible to that of his human pack *(you!)*. Just as we guide little children to learn our way of life, we must show the puppy when it is time to play, eat, sleep, exercise and even entertain himself.

Your puppy should always sleep in his crate. He should also learn that, during times of household confusion and excessive human activity such as at breakfast when family members are preparing for the day, he can play by himself in relative safety and comfort in his designated area. Each time you leave the puppy alone, he should understand exactly where he is to stay. Puppies are chewers. They cannot tell the difference between lamp cords, television wires, shoes, table legs, etc. Chewing into a television wire, for example, can be fatal to the puppy while a shorted wire can start a fire in the house.

If the puppy chews on the

puppy to lie down and stretch out as well as stand up without rubbing his head on the top, yet small enough so that he cannot relieve himself at one end and sleep at the other without coming into contact with his droppings until fully trained to relieve himself outside. The designated area should be lined with clean bedding and a toy. Water must always be available, in a non-spill container.

Dogs are, by nature, clean animals and will not remain close to their relief areas unless forced to do so. In those cases, they then become dirty dogs and usually remain that way for life.

Wire crates are usually available at pet shops in a KD (knocked-down) version. Be sure there is a suitable location for a stable water supply.

At 11 weeks of age, this Cairn required 10 relief trips per day! Keep a close eye on your puppy to avoid his having an accident indoors.

arm of the chair when he is alone, you would probably discipline him angrily when you get home. Thus, he makes the association that your coming home means he is going to be punished. (He will not remember chewing up the chair and is incapable of making the association of the discipline with his naughty deed.)

Other times of excitement, such as visits, family parties, etc., can be fun for the puppy providing he can view the activities from the security of his designated area. He is not underfoot and he is not being fed all sorts of tidbits that will probably cause him stomach distress, yet he still feels a part of the fun.

SCHEDULE

A puppy should be taken to his relief area each time he is released from his designated area, after meals, after play sessions, when he first awakens in the morning (at age eight weeks, this can mean 5 a.m.!). The puppy will indicate that he's ready "to go" by circling or sniffing busily—do not misinterpret these signs. For a puppy less than ten weeks of age, a routine of taking him out every hour is necessary. As the puppy grows, he will be able to wait for longer periods of time.

Keep trips to his relief area

HOW MANY TIMES A DAY?

AGE	RELIEF TRIPS
To 14 weeks	10
14–22 weeks	8
22–32 weeks	6
Adulthood (dog stops growing)	4

These are estimates, of course, but they are a guide to the *minimum* number of opportunities a dog should have each day to relieve himself.

short. Stay no more than five or six minutes and then return to the house. If he goes during that time, praise him lavishly and take him indoors immediately. If he does not, but he has an accident when you go back indoors, pick him up immedi-

Always clean up after your dog, whether you're in a public place or your own yard.

THE SUCCESS METHOD

Success that comes by luck is usually short-lived. Success that comes by well-thought-out proven methods is often more easily achieved and permanent. This is the Success Method. It is designed to give you, the puppy owner, a simple yet proven way to help your puppy develop clean living habits and a feeling of security in his new environment.

6 Steps to Successful Crate Training

1 Tell the puppy "Crate time!" and place him in the crate with a small treat (a piece of cheese or half of a biscuit). Let him stay in the crate for five minutes while you are in the same room. Then release him and praise lavishly. Never release him when he is fussing. Wait until he is quiet before you let him out.

2 Repeat Step 1 several times a day.

3 The next day, place the puppy in the crate as before. Let him stay there for ten minutes. Do this several times.

4 Continue building time in five-minute increments until the puppy stays in his crate for 30 minutes with you in the room. Always take him to his relief area after prolonged periods in his crate.

5 Now go back to Step 1 and let the puppy stay in his crate for five minutes, this time while you are out of the room.

6 Once again, build crate time in five-minute increments with you out of the room. When the puppy will stay willingly in his crate (he may even fall asleep!) for 30 minutes with you out of the room, he will be ready to stay in it for several hours at a time.

ately, say "No! No!" and return to his relief area. Wait a few minutes, then return to the house again. Never hit a puppy or rub his face in urine or excrement when he has an accident!

Once indoors, put the puppy in his crate until you have had time to clean up his accident. Then release him to the family area and watch him more closely than before. Chances are, his accident was a result of your not picking up his signal or waiting too long before offering him the opportunity to relieve himself. Never hold a grudge against the puppy for accidents.

Let the puppy learn that going outdoors means it is time to relieve himself, not play. Once trained, he will be able to play indoors and out and still differentiate between the times for play versus the times for relief.

Help him develop regular hours for naps, being alone, playing by himself and just resting, all in his crate. Encourage him to entertain himself while you are busy with your activities. Let him learn that having you near is comforting, but it is not your main purpose in life to provide him with undivided attention.

Each time you put a puppy in his own area, use the same command, whatever suits best. Soon, he will run to his crate or special area when he hears you say those words. Crate training provides safety for you, the puppy and the home. It also provides the puppy with a feeling of security, and that helps the puppy achieve self-confidence and clean habits. Remember that one of the primary ingredients in house-training your puppy is control. Regardless of your lifestyle, there will always be occasions when you will need to have a place where your dog can stay and be happy and safe. Crate training is the answer for now and in the future.

In conclusion, a few key elements are really all you need for a successful house-training method—consistency, frequency, praise, control and supervision.

PLAN TO PLAY

The puppy should also have regular play and exercise sessions when he is with you or a family member. Exercise for a very young puppy can consist of a short walk around the house or yard. Playing can include fetching games with a large ball or a special toy. (All puppies teethe and need soft things upon which to chew.)

Remember to restrict play periods to indoors within his living area (the family room, for example) until he is completely house-trained.

Eight weeks old and ready for a new life. Help him to develop a schedule of naps, meals, relief trips and play. He depends on you to help him to adjust to your life.

By following these procedures with a normal, healthy puppy, you and the puppy will soon be past the stage of accidents and ready to move on to a clean and rewarding life together.

ROLES OF DISCIPLINE, REWARD AND PUNISHMENT
Discipline, training one to act in accordance with rules, brings

order to life. It is as simple as that. Without discipline, particularly in a group society, chaos reigns supreme and the group will eventually perish. Humans and canines are social animals and need some form of discipline in order to function effectively. They must procure food, protect their home base, reproduce to keep the species going and guard their offspring.

If there were no discipline in the lives of social animals, they would eventually die from starvation and/or predation by other stronger animals. In the case of domestic canines, dogs need discipline in their lives in order to understand how their pack (you and other family members) functions and how they must act in order to survive.

KEEP SMILING
Never train your dog, puppy or adult, when you are angry or in a sour mood. Dogs are very sensitive to human feelings, especially anger, and if your dog senses that you are angry or upset, he will connect your anger with his training and learn to resent or fear his training sessions.

Digging holes in the sand in search of something edible...like sand crabs. Cairns are both diggers and natural hunters.

A large humane society in a highly populated area recently surveyed dog owners regarding their satisfaction with their relationships with their dogs. People who had trained their dogs were 75% more satisfied with their pets than those who had never trained their dogs.

Dr. Edward Thorndike, an animal psychologist, famous for his "trial and error learning" theory, stated that a behavior that results in a pleasant event tends to be repeated. Likewise, a behavior that results in an unpleasant event tends not to be repeated. It is this theory on which training methods are based today. For example, if you manipulate a dog to perform a specific behavior and reward him for doing it, he is likely to do it again because he enjoyed the end result.

Occasionally, punishment, a penalty inflicted for an offense, is necessary. The best type of punishment often comes from an outside source. For example, a child is told not to touch the stove because he may get burned. He disobeys and touches the stove. In doing so, he receives a burn. From that time on, he respects the heat of the stove and avoids contact with it. Therefore, a behavior that results in an unpleasant event tends not to be repeated.

A good example of a dog learning the hard way is the dog who chases the house cat. He is told many times to leave the cat alone, yet he persists in teasing the cat. Then, one day he begins chasing the cat but the cat turns and swipes a claw across the dog's face, leaving him with a painful gash on his nose. The final result is that the dog stops chasing the cat.

TRAINING EQUIPMENT

COLLAR AND LEAD

For a Cairn Terrier the collar and lead that you use for training must be one with which you are easily able to work, not too heavy for the dog and perfectly safe.

HE'S AN ORIGINAL

Dogs are as different from each other as people are. What works for one dog may not work for another. Have an open mind. If one method of training is unsuccessful, try another.

You can easily bribe your Cairn puppy using a tasty treat.

TREATS

Have a bag of treats on hand. Use a soft treat, a chunk of cheese or a piece of cooked chicken rather than a dry biscuit. By the time the dog has finished chewing a dry treat, he will forget why he is being rewarded in the first place! Keep in mind that using food rewards will not teach a dog to beg at the table—the only way to teach a dog to beg at the table is to give him food from the table. In training, rewarding the dog with a food treat will help him associate praise and the treats with learning new behaviors that obviously please his owner.

TRAINING BEGINS:
ASK THE DOG A QUESTION

In order to teach your dog anything, you must first get his attention. After all, he cannot learn anything if he is looking away from you with his mind on something else.

To get his attention, ask him "School?" and immediately walk over to him and give him a treat as you tell him "Good dog." Wait a minute or two and repeat the routine, this time with a treat in your hand as you approach within a foot of the dog. Do not go directly to him, but stop about a foot short of him and hold out the treat as you ask

him the treat and praise again.

By this time, the dog will probably be getting the idea that if he pays attention to you, especially when you ask that question, it will pay off in treats and fun activities for him. In other words, he learns that "school" means doing fun things with you that result in treats and positive attention for him.

Remember that the dog does not understand your verbal language, he only recognizes sounds. Your question translates to a series of sounds for him, and those sounds become the signal to go to you and pay attention; if he does, he will get to interact with you plus receive treats and praise.

Watching a treat in your hand, the Cairn is fully alert, wondering what your next move will be. He intends to please you so he can earn the treat. This is the basis of training with treats.

"School?" He will see you approaching with a treat in your hand and most likely begin walking toward you. As you meet, give him the treat and praise again.

The third time, ask the question, have a treat in your hand and walk only a short distance toward the dog so that he must walk almost all the way to you. As he reaches you, give

THE BASIC COMMANDS

TEACHING SIT

Now that you have the dog's attention, attach his lead and hold it in your left hand and a food treat in your right. Place your food hand at the dog's nose and let him lick the treat but not take it from you. Say "Sit" and slowly raise your food hand from in front of the dog's nose up over his head so that he is looking at the ceiling. As he bends his head upward, he will have to bend his knees to maintain his balance. As he bends his knees, he will assume a sit position. At that point, release the food treat and praise lavishly with comments such as "Good dog! Good sit!," etc. Remember to always praise

Once the Cairn assumes a proper sit position, make him hold it before rewarding him.

enthusiastically, because dogs relish verbal praise from their owners and feel so proud of themselves whenever they accomplish a behavior.

You will not use food forever in getting the dog to obey your commands. Food is only used to teach new behaviors, and once the dog knows what you want when you give a specific command, you will wean him off the food treats but still maintain the verbal praise. After all, you will always have your voice with you, and there will be many times when you have no food rewards but expect the dog to obey.

Puppies have a way of always being "underfoot." You don't want your Cairn chewing on your shoe laces, whether or not you are wearing the shoes!

TEACHING DOWN

Teaching the down exercise is easy when you understand how the dog perceives the down position, and it is very difficult when you do not. Dogs perceive the down position as a submissive one, therefore teaching the down exercise using a forceful method can sometimes make the dog develop such a fear of the

The dog is taught the down position from the sit position. Teaching down is not an easy exercise because dogs feel insecure in the down position.

down that he either runs away when you say "Down" or he attempts to snap at the person who tries to force him down.

Have the dog sit close alongside your left leg, facing in the same direction as you are. Hold the lead in your left hand and a food treat in your right. Now place your left hand lightly on the top of the dog's shoulders where they meet above the spinal cord. Do not push down on the dog's shoulders; simply rest your left hand there so you can guide the dog to lie down close to your left leg rather than to swing away from your side when he drops.

Now place the food hand at the dog's nose, say "Down" very softly (almost a whisper), and slowly lower the food hand to the dog's front feet. When the food hand reaches the floor, begin moving it forward along the floor in front of the dog. Keep talking softly to the dog, saying things like, "Do you want this treat? You can do this, good dog." Your reassuring tone of voice will help calm the dog as he tries to follow the food hand in order to get the treat.

When the dog's elbows touch the floor, release the food and praise softly. Try to get the dog to maintain that down position for several seconds before you let him sit up again. The goal here is to get the dog to settle

> ### DOUBLE JEOPARDY
> A dog in jeopardy never lies down. He stays alert on his feet because instinct tells him that he may have to run away or fight for his survival. Therefore, if a dog feels threatened or anxious, he will not lie down. Consequently, it is important to keep the dog calm and relaxed as he learns the down exercise.

food and praise lavishly.

To teach the down/stay, do the down as previously described. As soon as the dog lies down, say "Stay" and step out on your right foot just as you did in the sit/stay. Count to five and then return to stand beside the dog with him on your left side. Release the treat and praise as always.

Within a week or ten days, you can begin to add a bit of distance between you and your dog when you leave him. When you do, use your left hand open with the palm facing the dog as a stay signal, much the same as the hand signal a police officer uses to stop traffic at an intersection. Hold the food treat in your right hand as before, but this time the food is not touching the dog's nose. He will watch the

down and not feel threatened in the down position.

TEACHING STAY
It is easy to teach the dog to stay in either a sit or a down position. Again, we use food and praise during the teaching process as we help the dog to understand exactly what it is that we are expecting him to do.

To teach the sit/stay, start with the dog sitting on your left side as before and hold the lead in your left hand. Have a food treat in your right hand and place your food hand at the dog's nose. Say "Stay" and step out on your right foot to stand directly in front of the dog, toe to toe, as he licks and nibbles the treat. Be sure to keep his head facing upward to maintain the sit position. Count to five and then swing around to stand next to the dog again with him on your left. As soon as you get back to the original position, release the

Teaching a dog to stay in the sit or down position is not difficult. This exercise increases your Cairn's patience and obedience.

A Cairn puppy is moldable and attentive. This eight-week-old toddler has just had his coat plucked for the first time.

not love the game or that fails to come when called. The secret, it seems, is never to teach the word "come."

At times when an owner most wants his dog to come when called, the owner is likely to be upset or anxious and he allows these feelings to come through in the tone of his voice when he calls his dog. Hearing that desperation in his owner's voice, the dog fears the results of going to him and therefore either disobeys outright or runs in the opposite direction. The secret, therefore, is to teach the dog a game and, when you want him to come to you, simply play the game. It is practically a no-fail solution!

To begin, have several members of your family take a few food treats and each go into a different room in the house. Take turns calling the dog, and each person should celebrate the

food hand and quickly learn that he is going to get that treat as soon as you return to his side.

When you can stand 1 yard away from your dog for 30 seconds, you can then begin building time and distance in both stays. Eventually, the dog can be expected to remain in the stay position for prolonged periods of time until you return to him or call him to you. Always praise lavishly when he stays.

TEACHING COME

If you make teaching "come" a fun experience, you should never have a "student" that does

---

"WHERE ARE YOU?"

When calling the dog, do not say "Come." Say things like, "Rover, where are you? See if you can find me! I have a biscuit for you!" Keep up a constant line of chatter with coaxing sounds and frequent questions such as, "Where are you?" The dog will learn to follow the sound of your voice to locate you and receive his reward.

"COME" ... BACK
Never call your dog to come to you for a correction or scold him when he reaches you. That is the quickest way to turn a come command into "Go away fast!" Dogs think only in the present tense, and your dog will connect the scolding with coming to you, not with the misbehavior of a few moments earlier.

dog's finding him with a treat and lots of happy praise. When a person calls the dog, he is actually inviting the dog to find him and get a treat as a reward for "winning."

A few turns of the "Where are you?" game and the dog will understand that everyone is playing the game and that each person has a big celebration awaiting his success at locating them. Once he learns to love the game, simply calling out "Where are you?" will bring him running from wherever he is when he hears that all-important question.

The come command is recognized as one of the most important things to teach a dog, but there are trainers who work with thousands of dogs and never teach the actual word "come." Yet these dogs will race to respond to a person who uses the dog's name followed by "Where are you?" For example, a woman has a 12-year-old companion dog who went blind, but who never fails to locate her owner when asked, "Where are you?"

Children particularly love to play this game with their dogs. Children can hide in smaller places like a shower stall or bathtub, behind a bed or under a table. The dog needs to work a little bit harder to find these hiding places, but when he does he loves to celebrate with a treat and a tussle with a favorite youngster.

TEACHING HEEL

Heeling means that the dog walks beside the owner without pulling. It takes time and patience on the owner's part to succeed at teaching the dog that he (the owner) will not proceed unless the dog is walking calmly

Your Cairn will stop what he's doing whenever he hears you call, "Where are you?"

All work and no play makes your Cairn a bored puppy. Incorporate some play time into your Cairn's lesson plans.

beside you for three steps without pulling, increase the number of steps you take to five. When he will walk politely beside you while you take five steps, you can increase the length of your walk to ten steps. Keep increasing the length of your stroll until the dog will walk quietly beside you without pulling as long as you want him to heel. When you stop heeling, indicate to the dog that the exercise is over by verbally praising as you pet him and say "OK, good dog." The "OK" is used as a release word, meaning that the exercise is finished and the dog is free to relax.

If you are dealing with a dog who insists on pulling you around, simply "put on your brakes" and stand your ground until the dog realizes that the two of you are not going anywhere until he is beside you and moving at your pace, not his. It may take some time just standing there to convince the

beside him. Pulling out ahead on the lead is definitely not acceptable.

Begin with holding the lead in your left hand as the dog sits beside your left leg. Move the loop end of the lead to your right hand but keep your left hand short on the lead so it keeps the dog in close next to you.

Say "Heel" and step forward on your left foot. Keep the dog close to you and take three steps. Stop and have the dog sit next to you in what we now call the heel position. Praise verbally, but do not touch the dog. Hesitate a moment and begin again with "Heel," taking three steps and stopping, at which point the dog is told to sit again.

Your goal here is to have the dog walk those three steps without pulling on the lead. When he will walk calmly

TUG OF WALK?

If you begin teaching the heel by taking long walks and letting the dog pull you along, he misinterprets this action as an acceptable form of taking a walk. When you pull back on the leash to counteract his pulling, he reads that tug as a signal to pull even harder!

HEELING WELL
Teach your dog to heel in an enclosed area. Once you think the dog will obey reliably and you want to attempt advanced obedience exercises such as off-lead heeling, test him in a fenced-in area so he cannot run away.

dog that you are the leader and you will be the one to decide on the direction and speed of your travel.

Each time the dog looks up at you or slows down to give a slack lead between the two of you, quietly praise him and say, "Good heel. Good dog." Eventually, the dog will begin to respond and within a few days he will be walking politely beside you without pulling on the lead. At first, the training sessions should be kept short and very positive; soon the dog will be able to walk nicely with you for increasingly longer distances. Remember also to give the dog free time and the opportunity to run and play when you have finished heel practice.

WEANING OFF FOOD IN TRAINING

Food is used in training new behaviors. Once the dog understands what behavior goes with a specific command, it is time to start weaning him off the food treats. At first, give a treat after each exercise. Then, start to give a treat only after every other exercise. Mix up the times when you offer a food reward and the times when you only offer praise so that the dog will never know when he is going to receive both food and praise and when he is going to receive only praise. This is called a variable-ratio reward system and it proves successful because there is always the chance that the owner will produce a treat, so the dog never stops trying for that reward. No matter what, *always* give verbal praise.

Heel training pays off on a daily basis, for pet dogs and show dogs alike.

OBEDIENCE CLASSES

It is a good idea to enroll in an obedience class if one is available in your area. If yours is a show dog, handling classes would be more appropriate. Many areas have dog clubs that offer basic obedience training as well as preparatory classes for obedience competition. There are also local dog trainers who offer similar classes.

At obedience trials, dogs can earn titles at various levels of competition. The beginning levels of competition include basic behaviors such as sit, down, heel, etc. The more advanced levels of competition include jumping, retrieving, scent discrimination and signal work. The advanced levels require a dog and owner to put a lot of time and effort into their training and the titles that can be earned at these levels of competition are very prestigious.

OTHER ACTIVITIES FOR LIFE

Whether a dog is trained in the structured environment of a class or alone with his owner at home, there are many activities that can bring fun and rewards to both owner and dog once they have mastered basic control. Teaching the dog to help out around the home, in the yard or on the farm provides great satisfaction to both dog and owner. In addition, the dog's help makes life a little easier for his owner and raises his stature as a valued companion to his family. It helps give the dog a purpose by occupying his mind and providing an outlet for his energy.

Backpacking is an exciting and healthful activity that the dog can be taught without assistance from more than his owner. The exercise of walking and climbing is good for man and dog alike, and the bond that they develop together is priceless.

If you are interested in participating in organized

OBEDIENCE SCHOOL

A basic obedience beginner's class usually lasts for six to eight weeks. Dog and owner attend an hour-long lesson once a week and practice for a few minutes, several times a day, each day at home. If done properly, the whole procedure will result in a well-mannered dog and an owner who delights in living with a pet that is eager to please and enjoys doing things with his owner.

competition with your Cairn Terrier, there are activities other than obedience in which you and your dog can become involved. Agility is a popular and fun sport where dogs run through an obstacle course that includes various jumps, tunnels and other exercises to test the dog's speed and coordination. The owners run through the course beside their dogs to give commands and to guide them through the course. Although competitive, the focus is on fun—it's fun to do, fun to watch, and great exercise.

A BORN PRODIGY

Occasionally, a dog and owner who have not attended formal classes have been able to earn entry-level obedience titles by obtaining competition rules and regulations from a local kennel club and practicing on their own to a degree of perfection. Obtaining the higher level titles, however, almost always requires extensive training under the tutelage of experienced instructors. In addition, the more difficult levels require more specialized equipment whereas the lower levels do not.

A game of fetch on the shore is every Cairn's idea of time well spent.

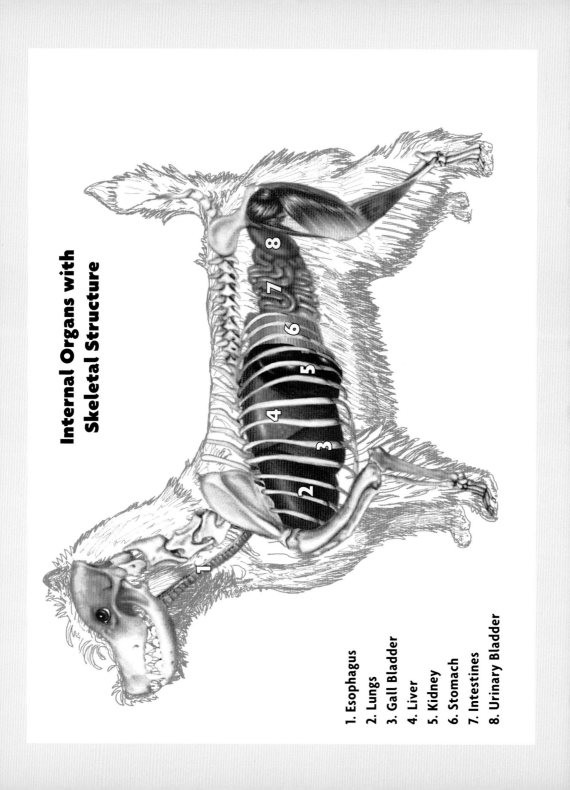

Internal Organs with Skeletal Structure

1. Esophagus
2. Lungs
3. Gall Bladder
4. Liver
5. Kidney
6. Stomach
7. Intestines
8. Urinary Bladder

Dogs suffer from many of the same physical illnesses as people. They might even share many of the same psychological problems. Since people usually know more about human diseases than canine maladies, many of the terms used in this chapter will be familiar but not necessarily those used by veterinarians. We will use the term *x-ray*, instead of the more acceptable term *radiograph*. We will also use the familiar term *symptoms* even though dogs don't have symptoms, which are verbal descriptions of the patient's feelings; dogs have *clinical signs*. Since dogs can't speak, we have to look for clinical signs...but we still use the term *symptoms* in this book.

As a general rule, medicine is *practiced*. That term is not arbitrary. Medicine is a constantly changing art as we learn more and more about genetics, electronic aids (like CAT scans and MRIs) and daily laboratory advances. There are many dog maladies, like canine hip dysplasia, which are not universally treated in the same manner. Some veterinarians opt for surgery more often than others do.

SELECTING A QUALIFIED VET

Your selection of a veterinarian should be based not only upon personality and ability with small dogs but also upon his convenience to your home. You want a vet who is close because you might have emergencies or need to make multiple visits for treatments. You want a vet who has services that you might require, such as tattooing and grooming facilities, as well as sophisticated pet supplies and a good reputation for ability and responsiveness. There is nothing more frustrating than

A qualified veterinarian is able to provide your Cairn Terrier with all the care he requires, including recommendations for specialized testing and treatment.

Breakdown of Veterinary Income by Category

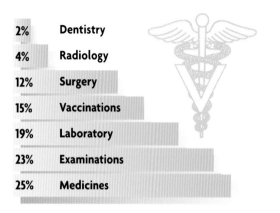

2%	Dentistry
4%	Radiology
12%	Surgery
15%	Vaccinations
19%	Laboratory
23%	Examinations
25%	Medicines

A typical vet's income, categorized according to services performed. This survey dealt with small-animal (pets) practices.

having to wait a day or more to get a response from your veterinarian.

All veterinarians are licensed and their diplomas and/or certificates should be displayed in their waiting rooms. There are, however, many veterinary specialties that usually require further studies and internships. There are specialists in heart problems (veterinary cardiologists), skin problems (veterinary dermatologists), teeth and gum problems (veterinary dentists), eye problems (veterinary ophthalmologists), x-rays (veterinary radiologists) and vets who have specialties in bones, muscles or certain organs. Most veterinarians do routine surgery such as neutering, stitching up wounds and docking tails. When the problem affecting your dog is serious, it is not unusual or impudent to get

another medical opinion, although it is courteous to advise the vets concerned about this. You might also want to compare costs among several veterinarians. Sophisticated health care and veterinary services are very costly. Don't be bashful about discussing these costs with your veterinarian or his staff. It is not infrequent that important decisions are based upon financial considerations.

PREVENTATIVE MEDICINE
It is much easier, less costly and more effective to practice preventative medicine than to fight bouts of illness and disease. Properly bred puppies come from parents that were selected based upon their genetic-disease profile. Their mother should have been vaccinated, free of all internal and external parasites, and properly nourished. For these reasons, a visit to the veterinarian who cared

PUPPY VACCINATIONS
Your veterinarian will probably recommend that your puppy be fully vaccinated before you take him outside. There are airborne diseases, parasite eggs in the grass and unexpected visits from other dogs that might be dangerous to your puppy's health. Other dogs are the most harmful reservoir of pathogenic organisms, as everything they have can be transmitted to your puppy.

First Aid at a Glance

Burns
Place the affected area under cool water; use ice if only a small area is burnt.

Bee stings/Insect bites
Apply ice to relieve swelling; antihistamine dosed properly.

Animal bites
Clean any bleeding area; apply pressure until bleeding subsides; go to the vet.

Spider bites
Use cold compress and a pressurized pack to inhibit venom's spreading.

Antifreeze poisoning
Induce vomiting with hydrogen peroxide. Seek *immediate* veterinary help!

Fish hooks
Removal best handled by vet; hook must be cut in order to remove.

Snake bites
Pack ice around bite; contact vet quickly; identify snake for proper antivenin.

Car accident
Move dog from roadway with blanket; seek veterinary aid.

Shock
Calm the dog; keep him warm; seek immediate veterinary help.

Nosebleed
Apply cold compress to the nose; apply pressure to any visible abrasion.

Bleeding
Apply pressure above the area; treat wound by applying a cotton pack.

Heat stroke
Submerge dog in cold bath; cool down with fresh air and water; go to the vet.

Frostbite/Hypothermia
Warm the dog with a warm bath, electric blankets or hot water bottles.

Abrasions
Clean the wound and wash out thoroughly with fresh water; apply antiseptic.

!! *Remember: an injured dog may attempt to bite a helping hand from fear and confusion. Always muzzle the dog before trying to offer assistance.* !!

for the dam is recommended. The dam can pass on disease resistance to her puppies, which can last for eight to ten weeks. She can also pass on parasites and many infections. That's why you should learn as much about the dam's health as possible.

WEANING TO FIVE MONTHS OLD
Puppies should be weaned by the time they are about two months old. A puppy that remains for at least eight weeks with his mother and littermates usually adapts better to other dogs and people later in his life.

Some new owners have their puppy examined by a veterinarian immediately, which is a good idea. Vaccination programs usually

> **CUSHING'S DISEASE**
> Cases of hyperactive adrenal glands (Cushing's disease) have been traced to the drinking of highly chlorinated water. Aerate or age your dog's drinking water before offering it.

begin when the puppy is very young.

The puppy will have his teeth examined and have his skeletal conformation and general health checked prior to certification by the veterinarian. Puppies in certain breeds have problems with their kneecaps, eye cataracts and other eye problems, heart murmurs and undescended testicles. They may also have personality problems and

At around five months of age, your Cairn puppy should be examined by the vet to determine how he's developing, in mind and body.

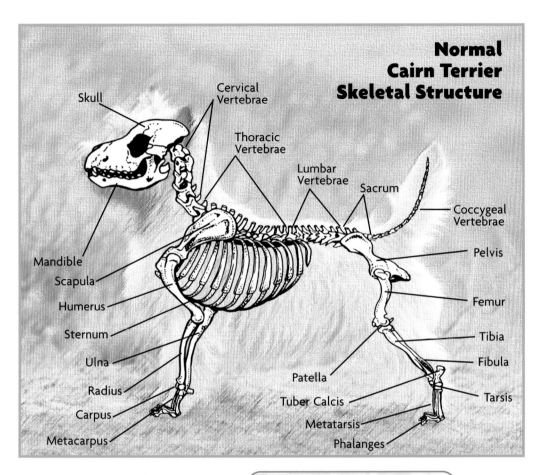

Normal Cairn Terrier Skeletal Structure

Skull
Cervical Vertebrae
Thoracic Vertebrae
Lumbar Vertebrae
Sacrum
Coccygeal Vertebrae
Pelvis
Mandible
Scapula
Humerus
Sternum
Ulna
Radius
Carpus
Metacarpus
Patella
Tuber Calcis
Metatarsis
Phalanges
Femur
Tibia
Fibula
Tarsis

your veterinarian might have training in temperament evaluation.

VACCINATION SCHEDULING
Most vaccinations are given by injection and should only be done by a veterinarian. Both he and you should keep a record of the date of the injection, the identification of the vaccine and the amount given. Some vets give a first vaccination at eight weeks, but most dog breeders prefer the course not to commence until

BE CAREFUL WHERE YOU WALK YOUR DOG
Dogs who have been exposed to lawns sprayed with herbicides have double and triple the rate of malignant lymphoma. Suburban dogs are especially at risk, as they are exposed to manicured lawns and gardens. Dogs perspire and absorb through their footpads. Be careful where your dog walks and always avoid any area that appears yellowed from chemical overspray. These chemicals are not good for you, either!

HEALTH AND VACCINATION SCHEDULE

AGE IN WEEKS:	6TH	8TH	10TH	12TH	14TH	16TH	20-24TH	52ND
Worm Control	✔	✔	✔	✔	✔	✔	✔	
Neutering							✔	
Heartworm		✔		✔		✔	✔	
Parvovirus	✔		✔		✔		✔	✔
Distemper		✔		✔		✔		✔
Hepatitis		✔		✔		✔		✔
Leptospirosis								✔
Parainfluenza	✔		✔		✔			✔
Dental Examination		✔					✔	✔
Complete Physical		✔					✔	✔
Coronavirus				✔			✔	✔
Canine Cough	✔							
Hip Dysplasia								✔
Rabies							✔	

Vaccinations are not instantly effective. It takes about two weeks for the dog's immune system to develop antibodies. Most vaccinations require annual booster shots. Your vet should guide you in this regard.

about ten weeks because of negating any antibodies passed on by the dam. The vaccination scheduling is usually based on a 15-day cycle. You must take your vet's advice as to when to vaccinate as this may differ according to the vaccine used. Most vaccinations immunize your puppy against viruses.

The usual vaccines contain immunizing doses of several different viruses such as distemper, parvovirus, parainfluenza and hepatitis. There are other vaccines available when the puppy is at risk.

You should rely upon professional advice. This is especially true for the booster-shot program. Most vaccination programs require a

VACCINE ALLERGIES

Vaccines do not work all the time. Sometimes dogs are allergic to them and many times the antibodies, which are supposed to be stimulated by the vaccine, just are not produced. You should keep your dog in the veterinary clinic for an hour after it is vaccinated to be sure there are no allergic reactions.

NEUTERING/SPAYING

Male dogs are castrated. The operation removes both testicles and requires that the dog be anesthetized. Recovery takes about one week. Females are spayed; in this operation, the uterus (womb) and both of the ovaries are removed. This is major surgery, also carried out under general anesthesia, and it usually takes a bitch two weeks to recover.

booster when the puppy is a year old and once a year thereafter. In some cases, circumstances may require more frequent immunizations. Canine cough, more formally known as tracheobronchitis, is treated with a vaccine that is sprayed into the dog's nostrils. Canine cough is usually included in routine vaccination, but this is often not so effective as for other major diseases.

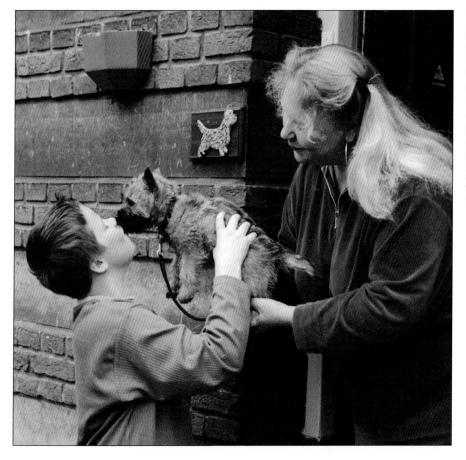

When you take your Cairn puppy home from the breeder, you should immediately visit your veterinarian to discuss your dog's present and future needs and to have your new puppy evaluated for possible health concerns.

FIVE MONTHS TO ONE YEAR OF AGE
Unless you intend to breed or show your dog, neutering the puppy at six months of age is recommended. Under no circumstances should a bitch be spayed prior to her first season. Discuss this with your veterinarian; most professionals advise neutering the puppy. Neutering/spaying has proven to be extremely beneficial to both male and female puppies. Besides eliminating the possibility of pregnancy and pyometra in bitches and testicular cancer in male dogs, it inhibits breast cancer in bitches and prostate cancer in male dogs.

DOGS OLDER THAN ONE YEAR
Continue to visit the veterinarian at least once a year. There is no such disease as old age, but bodily functions do change with age. The eyes and ears are no longer as efficient. Liver, kidney and intestinal functions often decline.

DISEASE REFERENCE CHART

	What is it?	What causes it?	Symptoms
Leptospirosis	Severe disease that affects the internal organs; can be spread to people.	A bacterium, which is often carried by rodents, that enters through mucous membranes and spreads quickly throughout the body.	Range from fever, vomiting and loss of appetite in less severe cases to shock, irreversible kidney damage and possibly death in most severe cases.
Rabies	Potentially deadly virus that infects warm-blooded mammals.	Bite from a carrier of the virus, mainly wild animals.	1st stage: dog exhibits change in behavior, fear. 2nd stage: dog's behavior becomes more aggressive. 3rd stage: loss of coordination, trouble with bodily functions.
Parvovirus	Highly contagious virus, potentially deadly.	Ingestion of the virus, which is usually spread through the feces of infected dogs.	Most common: severe diarrhea. Also vomiting, fatigue, lack of appetite.
Canine cough	Contagious respiratory infection.	Combination of types of bacteria and virus. Most common: *Bordetella bronchiseptica* bacteria and parainfluenza virus.	Chronic cough.
Distemper	Disease primarily affecting respiratory and nervous system.	Virus that is related to the human measles virus.	Mild symptoms such as fever, lack of appetite and mucus secretion progress to evidence of brain damage, "hard pad."
Hepatitis	Virus primarily affecting the liver.	Canine adenovirus type I (CAV-1). Enters system when dog breathes in particles.	Lesser symptoms include listlessness, diarrhea, vomiting. More severe symptoms include "blue-eye" (clumps of virus in eye).
Coronavirus	Virus resulting in digestive problems.	Virus is spread through infected dog's feces.	Stomach upset evidenced by lack of appetite, vomiting, diarrhea.

Proper dietary changes, recommended by your veterinarian, can make life more pleasant for the aging Cairn Terrier and you.

SKIN PROBLEMS IN CAIRN TERRIERS

Veterinarians are consulted by dog owners for skin problems more than for any other group of diseases or maladies. Dogs' skin is almost as sensitive as human skin and both suffer from almost the same ailments (though the occurrence of acne in dogs is rare!). For this reason, veterinary dermatology has developed into a specialty practiced by many veterinarians.

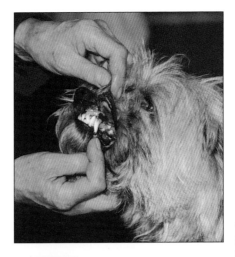

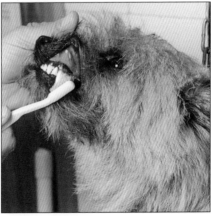

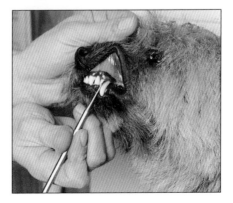

Your Cairn's well-being depends on his healthy teeth. Keep a close eye on his teeth and gums. A combination of home care and veterinary check-ups will protect your dog's teeth for life.

DENTAL HEALTH

A dental examination is in order when the dog is between six months and one year of age so that any permanent teeth that have erupted incorrectly can be corrected. It is important to begin a brushing routine at home, using dental-care products made for dogs, such as special toothbrushes and toothpaste. Durable nylon and safe edible chews should be a part of your puppy's arsenal for good health, good teeth and pleasant breath. The vast majority of dogs three to four years old and older has diseases of the gums from lack of dental attention. Using the various types of dental chews can be very effective in controlling dental plaque.

Since many skin problems have visual symptoms that are almost identical, it requires the skill of an experienced veterinary dermatologist to identify and cure many of the more severe skin disorders. Pet shops sell many treatments for skin problems but most of the treatments are directed at symptoms and not the underlying problem(s). If your dog is suffering from a skin disorder, you should seek professional assistance as quickly as possible. As with all diseases, the earlier a problem is identified and treated, the more successful is the cure.

Hereditary Skin Disorders

Veterinary dermatologists are currently researching a number of skin disorders that are believed to have hereditary bases. These inherited diseases are transmitted by both parents, who appear (phenotypically) normal but have a recessive gene for the disease, meaning that they carry, but are not affected by, the disease. These diseases pose serious problems to breeders because in some instances there are no methods of identifying carriers. Often the secondary diseases associated with these skin conditions are even more debilitating than the skin disorders themselves, including cancers and respiratory problems.

Among the hereditary skin disorders, for which the mode of inheritance is known, are acrodermatitis, cutaneous asthenia (Ehlers-Danlos syndrome), sebaceous adenitis, cyclic hematopoiesis, dermatomyositis, IgA deficiency, color dilution alopecia and nodular dermatofibrosis. Some of these disorders are limited to one or two breeds, while others affect a large number of breeds. All inherited diseases must be diagnosed and treated by a veterinary specialist.

Parasite Bites

Many of us are allergic to insect bites. The bites itch, erupt and may even become infected. Dogs have the same reaction to fleas, ticks and/or mites. When an insect lands on you, you have the chance to whisk it away with your hand. Unfortunately, when your dog is bitten by a flea, tick or mite, he can only scratch it away or bite it. By the time the dog has

CARETAKER OF TEETH

You are your dog's caretaker and his dentist. Vets warn that plaque and tartar buildup on the teeth will damage the gums and allow bacteria to enter the dog's bloodstream, causing serious damage to the animal's vital organs. Studies show that over 50 percent of dogs have some form of gum disease before age three. Daily or weekly tooth cleaning (with a brush or soft gauze pad wipes) can add to your dog's life.

> **MORE THAN VACCINES**
>
> Vaccinations help prevent your new puppy from contracting diseases, but they do not cure them. Proper nutrition as well as parasite control keep your dog healthy and less susceptible to many dangerous diseases. Remember that your dog depends on you to ensure his well-being.

been bitten, the parasite has done some of its damage. It may also have laid eggs to cause further problems in the near future. The itching from parasite bites is probably due to the saliva injected into the site when the parasite sucks the dog's blood.

AUTO-IMMUNE SKIN CONDITIONS

Auto-immune skin conditions are commonly referred to as being allergic to yourself, while allergies are usually inflammatory reactions to an outside stimulus. Auto-immune diseases cause serious damage to the tissues that are involved.

The best known auto-immune disease is lupus, which affects people as well as dogs. The symptoms are variable and may affect the kidneys, bones, blood chemistry and skin. It can be fatal to both dogs and humans, though it is not thought to be transmissible. It is usually successfully treated with cortisone, prednisone or similar corticosteroid, but

Among the dangers that lurk in the woods— wolves, bears and goblins—are blood-sucking parasites like ticks.

> **FAT OR FICTION?**
> The myth that dogs need extra fat in their diets can be harmful. Should your vet recommend extra fat, use safflower oil instead of animal oils. Safflower oil has been shown to be less likely to cause allergic reactions.

extensive use of these drugs can have harmful side effects.

AIRBORNE ALLERGIES

Just as humans have hay fever, rose fever and other fevers from which they suffer during the pollinating season, many dogs suffer from the same allergies. When the pollen count is high, your dog might suffer but don't expect them to sneeze and have runny noses. Dogs react to pollen allergies the same way they react to fleas—they scratch and bite themselves.

Dogs, like humans, can be tested for allergens. Discuss the testing with your veterinary dermatologist.

FOOD PROBLEMS

FOOD ALLERGIES

Dogs can be allergic to many foods that are best-sellers and highly recommended by breeders and veterinarians. Changing the brand of food that you buy may not eliminate the problem if the element to which the dog is allergic is contained in the new brand.

Recognizing a food allergy is difficult. Humans vomit or have rashes when we eat a food to which we are allergic. Dogs neither vomit nor (usually) develop a rash. They react in the same manner as they do to an airborne or flea allergy: they itch, scratch and bite. Thus making the diagnosis extremely difficult. While pollen allergies and parasite bites are usually seasonal, food allergies are year-round problems.

FOOD INTOLERANCE

Food intolerance is the inability of the dog to completely digest certain foods. For example, puppies that may have done very well on their mother's milk may not do well on cow's milk. The result of this food intolerance may be loose bowels, passing gas and stomach pains. These are the only obvious symptoms of food intolerance and that makes diagnosis difficult.

TREATING FOOD PROBLEMS

It is possible to handle food allergies and food intolerance yourself. Put your dog on a diet that he has never had. Obviously if he has never eaten this new food he can't have been allergic or intolerant of it. Start with a single ingredient that is not in the dog's

Keep "people food" out of your Cairn's reach. No dog can resist stealing a tasty morsel, but these "treats" can give your pet an upset stomach.

diet at the present time. Ingredients like chopped beef or chicken are common in dog's diets, so try something like fish, lamb or any other animal-protein source. Keep the dog on this diet (with no additives) for a month. If the symptoms of food allergy or intolerance disappear, chances are your dog has a food allergy.

Don't think that the single ingredient cured the problem. You still must find a suitable diet and ascertain which ingredient in the old diet was objectionable. This is most easily done by adding ingredients to the new diet one at a time. Let the dog stay on the modified diet for a month before you add another ingredient. Eventually, you will determine the ingredient that caused the adverse reaction.

An alternative method is to carefully study the ingredients in the diet to which your dog is allergic or intolerant. Identify the main ingredient in this diet and eliminate the main ingredient by buying a different food that does not have that ingredient. Keep experimenting until the symptoms disappear after one month on the new diet.

HOMEOPATHY:
an alternative to conventional medicine

"Less is Most"

Using this principle, the strength of a homeopathic remedy is measured by the number of serial dilutions that were undertaken to create it. The greater the number of serial dilutions, the greater the strength of the homeopathic remedy. The potency of a remedy that has been made by making a dilution of 1 part in 100 parts (or 1/100) is 1c or 1cH. If this remedy is subjected to a series of further dilutions, each one being 1/100, a more dilute and stronger remedy is produced. If the remedy is diluted in this way six times, it is called 6c or 6cH. A dilution of 6c is 1 part in 1,000,000,000,000. In general, higher potencies in more frequent doses are better for acute symptoms and lower potencies in more infrequent doses are more useful for chronic, long-standing problems.

CURING OUR DOGS NATURALLY

Holistic medicine means treating the whole animal as a unique, perfect, living being. Generally, holistic treatments do not suppress the symptoms that the body naturally produces, as do most medications prescribed by conventional doctors and vets. Holistic methods seek to cure disease by regaining balance and harmony in the patient's environment. Some of these methods include use of nutritional therapy, herbs, flower essences, aromatherapy, acupuncture, massage, chiropractic and, of course, the most popular holistic approach, homeopathy.

Homeopathy is a theory or system of treating illness with small doses of substances which, if administered in larger quantities, would produce the symptoms that the patient already has. This approach is often described as "like cures like." Although modern veterinary medicine is geared toward the "quick fix," homeopathy relies on the belief that, given the time, the body is able to heal itself and return to its natural, healthy state.

Choosing a remedy to cure a problem in our dogs is the difficult part of homeopathy. Consult with your vet for a professional diagnosis of your dog's symptoms. Often these symptoms

require immediate conventional care. If your vet is willing and knowledgeable, you may attempt a homeopathic remedy. Be aware that cortisone prevents homeopathic remedies from working. There are hundreds of possibilities and combinations to cure many problems in dogs, from basic physical problems such as excessive shedding, fleas or other parasites, unattractive doggy odor, bad breath, upset tummy, obesity, dry, oily or dull coat, diarrhea, ear problems or eye discharge (including tears and dry or mucousy matter), to behavioral abnormalities such as fear of loud noises, habitual licking, poor appetite, excessive barking and various phobias. From alumina to zincum metallicum, the remedies span the planet and the imagination...from flowers and weeds to chemicals, insect droppings, diesel smoke and volcanic ash.

Using "Like to Treat Like"

Unlike conventional medicines that suppress symptoms, homeopathic remedies treat illnesses with small doses of substances that, if administered in larger quantities, would produce the symptoms that the patient already has. While the same homeopathic remedy can be used to treat different symptoms in different dogs, here are some interesting remedies and their uses.

Apis Mellifica
(made from honey bee venom) can be used for allergies or to reduce swelling that occurs in acutely infected kidneys.

Diesel Smoke
can be used to help control travel sickness.

Calcarea Fluorica
(made from calcium fluoride, which helps harden bone structure) can be useful in treating hard lumps in tissues.

Natrum Muriaticum
(made from common salt, sodium chloride) is useful in treating thin, thirsty dogs.

Nitricum Acidum
(made from nitric acid) is used for symptoms you would expect to see from contact with acids, such as lesions, especially where the skin joins the linings of body orifices or openings such as the lips and nostrils.

Symphytum
(made from the herb Knitbone, *Symphytum officianale*) is used to encourage bones to heal.

Urtica Urens
(made from the common stinging nettle) is used in treating painful, irritating rashes.

HOMEOPATHIC REMEDIES FOR YOUR DOG

Symptom/Ailment	Possible Remedy
ALLERGIES	Apis Mellifica 30c, Astacus Fluviatilis 6c, Pulsatilla 30c, Urtica Urens 6c
ALOPECIA	Alumina 30c, Lycopodium 30c, Sepia 30c, Thallium 6c
ANAL GLANDS (BLOCKED)	Hepar Sulphuris Calcareum 30c, Sanicula 6c, Silicea 6c
ARTHRITIS	Rhus Toxicodendron 6c, Bryonia Alba 6c
CANINE COUGH	Drosera 6c, Ipecacuanha 30c
CATARACT	Calcarea Carbonica 6c, Conium Maculatum 6c, Phosphorus 30c, Silicea 30c
CONSTIPATION	Alumina 6c, Carbo Vegetabilis 30c, Graphites 6c, Nitricum Acidum 30c, Silicea 6c
COUGHING	Aconitum Napellus 6c, Belladonna 30c, Hyoscyamus Niger 30c, Phosphorus 30c
DIARRHEA	Arsenicum Album 30c, Aconitum Napellus 6c, Chamomilla 30c, Mercurius Corrosivus 30c
DRY EYE	Zincum Metallicum 30c
EAR PROBLEMS	Aconitum Napellus 30c, Belladonna 30c, Hepar Sulphuris 30c, Tellurium 30c, Psorinum 200c
EYE PROBLEMS	Borax 6c, Aconitum Napellus 30c, Graphites 6c, Staphysagria 6c, Thuja Occidentalis 30c
GLAUCOMA	Aconitum Napellus 30c, Apis Mellifica 6c, Phosphorus 30c
HEAT STROKE	Belladonna 30c, Gelsemium Sempervirens 30c, Sulphur 30c
HICCOUGHS	Cinchona Deficinalis 6c
HIP DYSPLASIA	Colocynthis 6c, Rhus Toxicodendron 6c, Bryonia Alba 6c
INCONTINENCE	Argentum Nitricum 6c, Causticum 30c, Conium Maculatum 30c, Pulsatilla 30c, Sepia 30c
INSECT BITES	Apis Mellifica 30c, Cantharis 30c, Hypericum Perforatum 6c, Urtica Urens 30c
ITCHING	Alumina 30c, Arsenicum Album 30c, Carbo Vegetabilis 30c, Hypericum Perforatum 6c, Mezerium 6c, Sulphur 30c
MASTITIS	Apis Mellifica 30c, Belladonna 30c, Urtica Urens 1m
MOTION SICKNESS	Cocculus 6c, Petroleum 6c
PATELLAR LUXATION	Gelsemium Sempervirens 6c, Rhus Toxicodendron 6c
PENIS PROBLEMS	Aconitum Napellus 30c, Hepar Sulphuris Calcareum 30c, Pulsatilla 30c, Thuja Occidentalis 6c
PUPPY TEETHING	Calcarea Carbonica 6c, Chamomilla 6c, Phytolacca 6c

The hairs of a Cairn Terrier. These are healthy hairs with intact cuticles (outer cover). This scanning electron micrograph (S.E.M.) has enlarged the hairs to 350 times the natural size.

S. E. M. BY DR DENNIS KUNKEL, UNIVERSITY OF HAWAII

A male dog flea, *Ctenocephalides canis*.

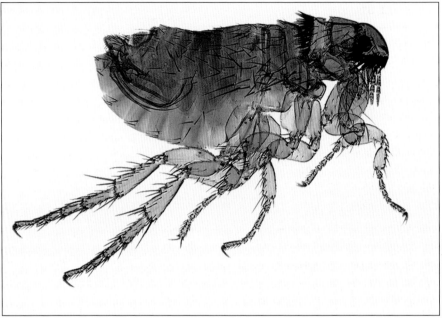

PHOTO BY JEAN CLAUDE REVY/PHOTOTAKE.

EXTERNAL PARASITES

FLEAS

Of all the problems to which dogs are prone, none is more well known and frustrating than fleas. Flea infestation is relatively simple to cure but difficult to

FLEA KILLER CAUTION— "POISON"

Flea-killers are poisonous. You should not spray these toxic chemicals on areas of a dog's body that he licks, including his genitals and his face. Flea killers taken internally are a better answer, but check with your vet in case internal therapy is not advised for your dog.

prevent. Parasites that are harbored inside the body are a bit more difficult to eradicate but they are easier to control.

To control flea infestation, you have to understand the flea's life cycle. Fleas are often thought of as a summertime problem, but centrally heated homes have changed the patterns and fleas can be found at any time of the year. The most effective method of flea control is a two-stage approach: one stage to kill the adult fleas, and the other to control the development of pre-adult fleas. Unfortunately, no single active ingredient is effective against all stages of the life cycle.

LIFE CYCLE STAGES

During its life, a flea will pass through four life stages: egg, larva, pupa or nymph and adult. The adult stage is the most visible and irritating stage of the flea life cycle, and this is why the majority of flea-control products concentrate on this stage. The fact is that adult fleas account for only 1% of the total flea population, and the other 99% exist in pre-adult stages, i.e., eggs, larvae and nymphs. The pre-adult stages are barely visible to the naked eye.

THE LIFE CYCLE OF THE FLEA

Eggs are laid on the dog, usually in quantities of about 20 or 30, several times a day. The adult female flea must have a blood meal before each egg-laying session. When first laid, the eggs will cling to the dog's hair, as the eggs are still moist. However, they will quickly dry out and fall from the dog, especially if the dog moves around or scratches. Many eggs will fall off in the dog's favorite area or an area in which he spends a lot of time, such as his bed.

Once the eggs fall from the dog onto the carpet or furniture, they will hatch into larvae. This takes from one to ten days. Larvae are not particularly mobile and will usually travel only a few inches from where they hatch. However, they do have a tendency to move away from bright light and heavy

---

EN GARDE:
CATCHING FLEAS OFF GUARD!
Consider the following ways to arm yourself against fleas:
- Add a small amount of pennyroyal or eucalyptus oil to your dog's bath. These natural remedies repel fleas.
- Supplement your dog's food with fresh garlic (minced or grated) and a hearty amount of brewer's yeast, both of which ward off fleas.
- Use a flea comb on your dog daily. Submerge fleas in a cup of bleach to kill them quickly.
- Confine the dog to only a few rooms to limit the spread of fleas in the home.
- Vacuum daily...and get all of the crevices! Dispose of the bag every few days until the problem is under control.
- Wash your dog's bedding daily. Cover cushions where your dog sleeps with towels, and wash the towels often.

---

traffic—under furniture and behind doors are common places to find high quantities of flea larvae.

The flea larvae feed on dead organic matter, including adult flea feces, until they are ready to change into adult fleas. Fleas will usually remain as larvae for around seven days. After this period, the larvae will pupate into protective pupae. While inside the pupae, the larvae will undergo metamorphosis and change into adult fleas. This can take as little time as a few days, but the adult fleas can remain inside the pupae waiting to hatch for up to two years. The pupae are signaled to hatch by certain stimuli, such as physical pressure—the pupae's being stepped on, heat from an animal's lying on the pupae or increased carbon-dioxide levels and vibrations—indicating that a suitable host is available.

Once hatched, the adult flea must feed within a few days. Once the adult flea finds a host, it will not leave voluntarily. It only becomes dislodged by grooming or the host animal's scratching.

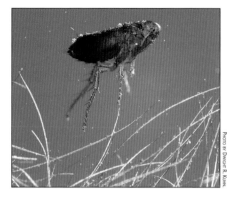

PHOTO BY DWIGHT R. KUHN

The adult flea will remain on the host for the duration of its life unless forcibly removed.

TREATING THE ENVIRONMENT AND THE DOG

Treating fleas should be a two-pronged attack. First, the environment needs to be treated; this includes carpets and furniture, especially the dog's bedding and areas underneath furniture. The environment should be treated with a household spray containing an Insect Growth Regulator (IGR) and an insecticide to kill the adult fleas. Most IGRs are effective against eggs and larvae; they actually mimic the fleas' own hormones and stop the eggs and larvae from developing into adult fleas. There are currently no treatments available to attack the pupa stage of the life cycle, so the adult insecticide is used to kill the newly hatched adult fleas before they find a host. Most IGRs are active for many months, while

S. E. M. BY DR. DENNIS KUNKEL, UNIVERSITY OF HAWAII

THE LIFE CYCLE OF THE FLEA

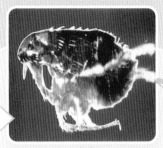

Adult

**Pupa
or
Nymph**

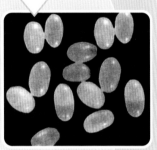

Egg

Larva

Fleas have been around for millions of years and have adapted to changing host animals. They are able to go through a complete life cycle in less than one month or they can extend their lives to almost two years by remaining as pupae or cocoons. They do not need blood or any other food for up to 20 months.

INSECT GROWTH REGULATOR (IGR)

Two types of products should be used when treating fleas—a product to treat the pet and a product to treat the home. Adult fleas represent less than 1% of the flea population. The pre-adult fleas (eggs, larvae and pupae) represent more than 99% of the flea population and are found in the environment; it is in the case of pre-adult fleas that products containing an Insect Growth Regulator (IGR) should be used in the home.

IGRs are a new class of compounds used to prevent the development of insects. They do not kill the insect outright, but instead use the insect's biology against it to stop it from completing its growth. Products that contain methoprene are the world's first and leading IGRs. Used to control fleas and other insects, this type of IGR will stop flea larvae from developing and protect the house for up to seven months.

The American dog tick, *Dermacentor variabilis*, is probably the most common tick found on dogs. Look at the strength in its eight legs! No wonder it's hard to detach them.

adult insecticides are only active for a few days.

When treating with a household spray, it is a good idea to vacuum before applying the product. This stimulates as many pupae as possible to hatch into adult fleas. The vacuum cleaner should also be treated with an insecticide to prevent the eggs and larvae that have been collected in the vacuum bag from hatching.

The second stage of treatment is to apply an adult insecticide to the dog. Traditionally, this would be in the form of a collar or a spray, but more recent innovations include digestible insecticides that poison the fleas when they ingest the dog's blood. Alternatively, there are drops that, when placed on the back of the dog's neck, spread throughout the hair and skin to kill adult fleas.

TICKS

Though not as common as fleas, ticks are found all over the tropical and temperate world. They don't bite, like fleas; they harpoon. They dig their sharp proboscis (nose) into the dog's skin and drink the blood. Their

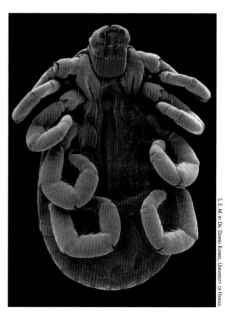

S. E. M. BY DR. DENNIS KUNKEL, UNIVERSITY OF HAWAII

only food and drink is dog's blood. Dogs can get Lyme disease, Rocky Mountain spotted fever, tick bite paralysis and many other diseases from ticks. They may live where fleas are found and they like to hide in cracks or seams in walls. They are controlled the same way fleas are controlled.

The American dog tick, *Dermacentor variabilis*, may well be the most common dog tick in many geographical areas, especially those areas where the climate is hot and humid. Most dog ticks have life expectancies of a week to six months, depending upon climatic conditions. They can neither jump nor fly, but they can crawl slowly and can range up to 16 feet to reach a sleeping or unsuspecting dog.

MITES

Just as fleas and ticks can be problematic for your dog, mites can also lead to an itchy nuisance. Microscopic in size, mites are related to ticks and generally take up permanent residence on their host animal—in this case, your dog! The term *mange* refers to any infestation caused by one of the mighty mites, of which there are six varieties that concern dog owners.

Demodex mites cause a condition known as demodicosis

DEER-TICK CROSSING

The great outdoors may be fun for your dog, but it also is a home to dangerous ticks. Deer ticks carry a bacterium known as *Borrelia burgdorferi* and are most active in the autumn and spring. When infections are caught early, penicillin and tetracycline are effective antibiotics, but, if left untreated, the bacteria may cause neurological, kidney and cardiac problems as well as long-term trouble with walking and painful joints.

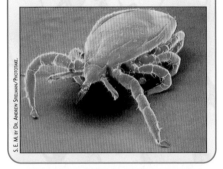

S. E. M. BY DR. ANDREW SPIELMAN/PHOTOTAKE.

PHOTO BY DR. DENNIS KUNKEL, UNIVERSITY OF HAWAII.

The head of an American dog tick, *Dermacentor variabilis*, enlarged and colorized for effect.

The mange mite, *Psoroptes bovis*, can infest cattle and other domestic animals.

Human lice look like dog lice; the two are closely related.

PHOTO BY DWIGHT R. KUHN.

(sometimes called red mange or follicular mange), in which the mites live in the dog's hair follicles and sebaceous glands in larger-than-normal numbers. This type of mange is commonly passed from the dam to her puppies and usually shows up on the puppies' muzzles, though demodicosis is not transferable from one normal dog to another. Most dogs recover from this type of mange without any treatment, though topical therapies are commonly prescribed by the vet.

The *Cheyletiellosis* mite is the hook-mouthed culprit associated with "walking dandruff," a condition that affects dogs as well as cats and rabbits. This mite lives on the surface of the animal's skin and is readily transferable through direct or indirect contact with an affected animal. The dandruff is present in the form of scaly skin, which may or may not be itchy. If not treated, this mange can affect a whole kennel of dogs and can be spread to humans as well.

The *Sarcoptes* mite causes intense itching on the dog in the form of a condition known as scabies or sarcoptic mange. The cycle of the *Sarcoptes* mite lasts about three weeks, and the mites live in the top layer of the dog's skin (epidermis), preferably in areas with little hair. Scabies is highly contagious and can be passed to humans. Sometimes an allergic reaction to the mite worsens the severe itching associated with sarcoptic mange.

Ear mites, *Otodectes cynotis,* lead to otodectic mange, which most commonly affects the outer ear canal of the dog, though other areas can be affected as well. Dogs with ear-mite infestation commonly scratch at their ears, causing further irritation, and shake their heads. Dark brown droppings in the outer ear confirm the diagnosis. Your vet can prescribe a treatment to flush out the ears and kill any eggs in the ears. A complete month of treatment is necessary to cure the mange.

Two other mites, less common in dogs, include *Dermanyssus gallinae* (the poultry or red mite) and *Eutrombicula alfreddugesi* (the North American mite associated with trombiculidiasis or chigger infestation). The poultry mite frequently lives on chickens, but can transfer to dogs who spend time near farm animals. Chigger

---

DO NOT MIX

Never mix parasite-control products without first consulting your vet. Some products can become toxic when combined with others and can cause fatal consequences.

NOT A DROP TO DRINK

Never allow your dog to swim in polluted water or public areas where water quality can be suspect. Even perfectly clear water can harbor parasites, many of which can cause serious to fatal illnesses in canines. Areas inhabited by waterfowl and other wildlife are especially dangerous.

---

infestation affects dogs in the Central US who have exposure to woodlands. The types of mange caused by both of these mites are treatable by vets.

INTERNAL PARASITES

Most animals—fishes, birds and mammals, including dogs and humans—have worms and other parasites that live inside their bodies. According to Dr. Herbert R. Axelrod, the fish pathologist, there are two kinds of parasites: dumb and smart. The smart parasites live in peaceful cooperation with their hosts (symbiosis), while the dumb parasites kill their hosts. Most worm infections are relatively easy to control. If they are not controlled, they weaken the host dog to the point that other medical problems occur, but they do not kill the host as dumb parasites would.

A brown dog tick, *Rhipicephalus sanguineus,* is an uncommon but annoying tick found on dogs.

PHOTO BY CAROLINA BIOLOGICAL SUPPLY/PHOTOTAKE.

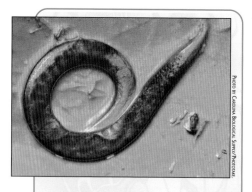

PHOTO BY CAROLINA BIOLOGICAL SUPPLY/PHOTOTAKE

The roundworm *Rhabditis* can infect both dogs and humans.

The roundworm, *Ascaris lumbricoides*.

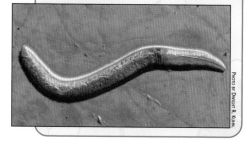

PHOTO BY DWIGHT R. KUHN

ROUNDWORMS

Average-size dogs can pass 1,360,000 roundworm eggs every day. For example, if there were only 1 million dogs in the world, the world would be saturated with thousands of tons of dog feces. These feces would contain around 15,000,000,000 roundworm eggs.

Up to 31% of home yards and children's sand boxes in the US contain roundworm eggs.

Flushing dog's feces down the toilet is not a safe practice because the usual sewage treatments do not destroy roundworm eggs.

Infected puppies start shedding roundworm eggs at three weeks of age. They can be infected by their mother's milk.

ROUNDWORMS

The roundworms that infect dogs are known scientifically as *Toxocara canis*. They live in the dog's intestines and shed eggs continually. It has been estimated that a dog produces about 6 or more ounces of feces every day. Each ounce of feces averages hundreds of thousands of roundworm eggs. There are no known areas in which dogs roam that do not contain roundworm eggs. The greatest danger of roundworms is that they infect people, too! It is wise to have your dog tested regularly for roundworms.

In young puppies, roundworms cause bloated bellies, diarrhea, coughing and vomiting, and are transmitted from the dam (through blood or milk). Affected puppies will not appear as animated as normal puppies. The worms appear spaghetti-like, measuring as long as 6 inches. Adult dogs can acquire roundworms through coprophagia (eating contaminated feces) or by killing rodents that carry roundworms.

Roundworm infection can kill puppies and cause severe problems in adults, as the hatched larvae travel to the lungs and trachea through the bloodstream. Cleanliness is the best preventative for roundworms. Always pick up after your dog and dispose of feces in appropriate receptacles.

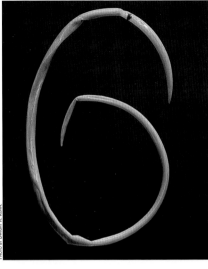

PHOTO BY DWIGHT R. KUHN.

HOOKWORMS

In the United States, dog owners have to be concerned about four different species of hookworm, the most common and most serious of which is *Ancylostoma caninum,* which prefers warm climates. The others are *Ancylostoma braziliense, Ancylostoma tubaeforme* and *Uncinaria stenocephala,* the latter of which is a concern to dogs living in the Northern US and Canada, as this species prefers cold climates. Hookworms are dangerous to humans as well as to dogs and cats, and can be the cause of severe anemia due to iron deficiency. The worm uses its teeth to attach itself to the dog's intestines and changes the site of its attachment about six times per day. Each time the worm repositions itself, the dog loses blood and can become anemic. *Ancylostoma caninum* is the most likely of the four species to cause anemia in the dog.

Symptoms of hookworm infection include dark stools, weight loss, general weakness, pale coloration and anemia, as well as possible skin problems. Fortunately, hookworms are easily purged from the affected dog with a number of medications that have proven effective. Discuss these with your vet. Most heartworm preventatives include a hookworm insecticide as well.

Owners also must be aware that hookworms can infect humans, who can acquire the larvae through exposure to contaminated feces. Since the worms cannot complete their life cycle on a human, the worms simply infest the skin and cause irritation. This condition is known as cutaneous larva migrans syndrome. As a preventative, use disposable gloves or a "poop-scoop" to pick up your dog's droppings and prevent your dog (or neighborhood cats) from defecating in children's play areas.

The hookworm, *Ancylostoma caninum.*

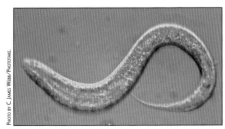

PHOTO BY C. JAMES WEBB/PHOTOTAKE.

The infective stage of the hookworm larva.

TAPEWORMS

Humans, rats, squirrels, foxes, coyotes, wolves and domestic dogs are all susceptible to tapeworm infection. Except in humans, tapeworms are usually not a fatal infection. Infected individuals can harbor 1000 parasitic worms.

Tapeworms, like some other types of worm, are hermaphroditic, meaning male and female in the same worm.

If dogs eat infected rats or mice, or anything else infected with tapeworm, they get the tapeworm disease. One month after attaching to a dog's intestine, the worm starts shedding eggs. These eggs are infective immediately. Infective eggs can live for a few months without a host animal.

The head and rostellum (the round prominence on the scolex) of a tapeworm, which infects dogs and humans.

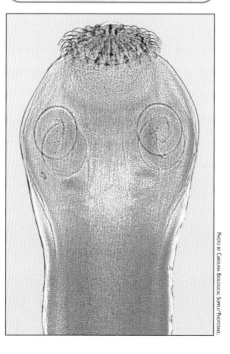

PHOTO BY CAROLINA BIOLOGICAL SUPPLY/PHOTOTAKE.

TAPEWORMS

There are many species of tapeworm, all of which are carried by fleas! The most common tapeworm affecting dogs is known as *Dipylidium caninum*. The dog eats the flea and starts the tapeworm cycle. Humans can also be infected with tapeworms—so don't eat fleas! Fleas are so small that your dog could pass them onto your hands, your plate or your food and thus make it possible for you to ingest a flea that is carrying tapeworm eggs.

While tapeworm infection is not life-threatening in dogs (smart parasite!), it can be the cause of a very serious liver disease for humans. About 50% of the humans infected with *Echinococcus multilocularis*, a type of tapeworm that causes alveolar hydatid, perish.

WHIPWORMS

In North America, whipworms are counted among the most common parasitic worms in dogs. The whipworm's scientific name is *Trichuris vulpis*. These worms attach themselves in the lower parts of the intestine, where they feed. Affected dogs may only experience upset tummies, colic and diarrhea. These worms, however, can live for months or years in the dog, beginning their larval stage in the small intestine, spending their adult stage in the large intestine and finally passing infective eggs through the dog's feces. The only way to detect whipworms is through a fecal examination, though this is not always foolproof. Treatment for whipworms is tricky, due to the worms' unusual life-cycle pattern, and very often dogs are reinfected due to exposure to infective eggs on the ground. The whipworm eggs can survive in the environment for as long as five years; thus, cleaning up droppings in your own backyard as well as in public places is absolutely essential for sanitation purposes and the health of your dog and others.

THREADWORMS
Though less common than roundworms, hookworms and those previously mentioned, threadworms concern dog owners in the Southwestern US and Gulf Coast area where the climate is hot and humid. Living in the small intestine of the dog, this worm measures a mere 2 millimeters and is round in shape. Like that of the whipworm, the threadworm's life cycle is very complex and the eggs and larvae are passed through the feces. A deadly disease in humans, *Strongyloides* readily infects people, and the handling of feces is the most common means of transmission. Threadworms are most often seen in young puppies; bloody diarrhea and pneumonia are symptoms. Sick puppies must be isolated and treated immediately; vets recommend a follow-up treatment one month later.

HEARTWORM PREVENTATIVES

There are many heartworm preventatives on the market, many of which are sold at your veterinarian's office. These products can be given daily or monthly, depending on the manufacturer's instructions. All of these preventatives contain chemical insecticides directed at killing heartworms, which leads to some controversy among dog owners. In effect, heartworm preventatives are necessary evils, though you should determine how necessary based on your pet's lifestyle. There is no doubt that heartworm is a dreadful disease that threatens the lives of dogs. However, the likelihood of your dog's being bitten by an infected mosquito is slim in most places, and a mosquito-repellent (or an herbal remedy such as Wormwood or Black Walnut) is much safer for your dog and will not compromise his immune system (the way heartworm preventatives will). Should you decide to use the traditional preventative "medications," you can consider giving the pill every other or third month. Since the toxins in the pill will kill the heartworms at all stages of development, the pill would be effective in killing larvae, nymphs or adults, and it takes four months for the larvae to reach the adult stage. Thus, there is no rationale to poisoning the dog's system on a monthly basis. Lastly, do not give the pill during the winter months, since there are no mosquitoes around to pass on their infection, unless you live in a tropical environment.

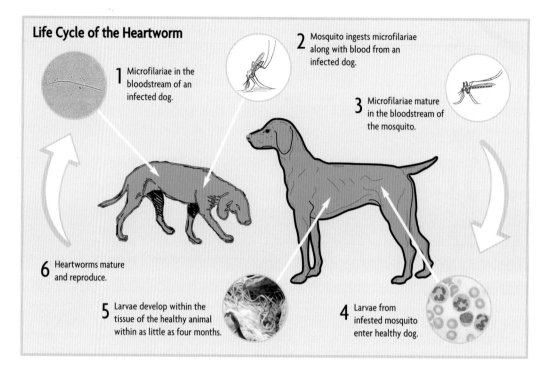

Life Cycle of the Heartworm

1 Microfilariae in the bloodstream of an infected dog.

2 Mosquito ingests microfilariae along with blood from an infected dog.

3 Microfilariae mature in the bloodstream of the mosquito.

4 Larvae from infested mosquito enter healthy dog.

5 Larvae develop within the tissue of the healthy animal within as little as four months.

6 Heartworms mature and reproduce.

HEARTWORMS

Heartworms are thin, extended worms up to 12 inches long, which live in a dog's heart and the major blood vessels surrounding it. Dogs may have up to 200 worms. Symptoms may be loss of energy, loss of appetite, coughing, the development of a pot belly and anemia.

Heartworms are transmitted by mosquitoes. The mosquito drinks the blood of an infected dog and takes in larvae with the blood. The larvae, called microfilariae, develop within the body of the mosquito and are passed on to the next dog bitten after the larvae mature. It takes two to three weeks for the larvae to develop to the infective stage within the body of the mosquito. Dogs are usually treated at about six weeks of age and maintained on a prophylactic dose given monthly.

Blood testing for heartworms is not necessarily indicative of how seriously your dog is infected. Although this is a dangerous disease, it is not easy for a dog to be infected. Discuss the various preventatives with your vet, as there are many different types now available. Together you can decide on a safe course of prevention for your dog.

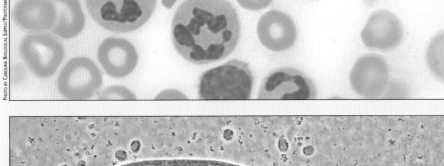

Magnified heartworm larvae, *Dirofilaria immitis.*

Heartworm, *Dirofilaria immitis.*

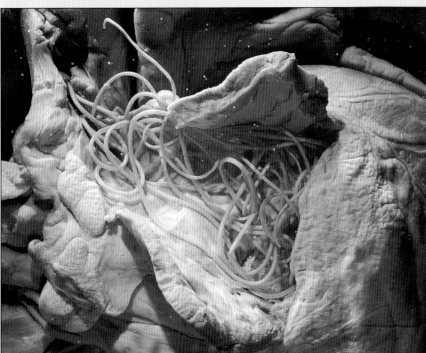

The heart of a dog infected with canine heartworm, *Dirofilaria immitis.*

CDS: COGNITIVE DYSFUNCTION SYNDROME
"Old-Dog Syndrome"

There are many ways for you to evaluate old-dog syndrome. Veterinarians have defined CDS (cognitive dysfunction syndrome) as the gradual deterioration of cognitive abilities. These are indicated by changes in the dog's behavior. When a dog changes his routine response, and maladies have been eliminated as the cause of these behavioral changes, then CDS is the usual diagnosis.

More than half the dogs over eight years old suffer from some form of CDS. The older the dog, the more chance he has of suffering from CDS. In humans, doctors often dismiss the CDS behavioral changes as part of "winding down."

There are four major signs of CDS: frequent potty accidents inside the home, sleeping much more or much less than normal, acting confused and failing to respond to social stimuli.

SYMPTOMS OF CDS

FREQUENT POTTY ACCIDENTS
- *Urinates in the house.*
- *Defecates in the house.*
- *Doesn't signal that he wants to go out.*

SLEEP PATTERNS
- *Awakens more slowly.*
- *Sleeps more than normal during the day.*
- *Sleeps less during the night.*

CONFUSION
- *Goes outside and just stands there.*
- *Appears confused with a faraway look in his eyes.*
- *Hides more often.*
- *Doesn't recognize friends.*
- *Doesn't come when called.*
- *Walks around listlessly and without a destination.*

FAILURE TO RESPOND TO SOCIAL STIMULI
- *Comes to people less frequently, whether called or not.*
- *Doesn't tolerate petting for more than a short time.*
- *Doesn't come to the door when you return home.*

CAIRN TERRIER

The term *old* is a qualitative term. For dogs, as well as their masters, old is relative. Certainly we can all distinguish between a puppy Cairn Terrier and an adult Cairn Terrier—there are the obvious physical traits, such as size, appearance and facial expressions, and personality traits. Puppies and young dogs like to play with children. Children's natural exuberance is a good match for the seemingly endless energy of young dogs. They like to run, jump, chase and retrieve. When dogs grow up and cease their interaction with children, they are often thought of as being too old to play with the kids.

On the other hand, if a Cairn Terrier is only exposed to people with less active lifestyles, his life will normally be less active and he will not seem to be getting old as his activity level slows down.

If people live to be 100 years old, dogs live to be 20 years old. While this is a good rule of thumb, it is very inaccurate. When trying to compare dog years to human years, you cannot make a generalization about all dogs. Terriers as a whole are long-lived dogs and your Cairn will be no different. If your dog lives to 8 years of age, he will often last until 12 years of age and sometimes even as long as 16

This delightful old girl exhibits the tell-tale signs of her senior hears: graying on her coat and a wisdom that is ineffable.

SENIOR SIGNS

An old dog starts to show one or more of the following symptoms:

- The hair on the face and paws starts to turn gray. The color breakdown usually starts around the eyes and mouth.
- Sleep patterns are deeper and longer, and the old dog is harder to awaken.
- Food intake diminishes.
- Responses to calls, whistles and other signals are ignored more and more.
- Eye contact does not evoke tail wagging (assuming it once did).

years of age. Give your dog his yearly inoculations, visit the veterinarian as needed, feed him a good diet and give him plenty of exercise and your dog should live a long life with you and give you much pleasure.

Dogs are generally considered mature within three years, but they can reproduce even earlier. So the first three years of a dog's life are like seven times that of comparable humans. That means a 3-year-old dog is like a 21-year-old human. As the curve of comparison shows, there is no hard and fast rule for comparing dog and human ages. The comparison is

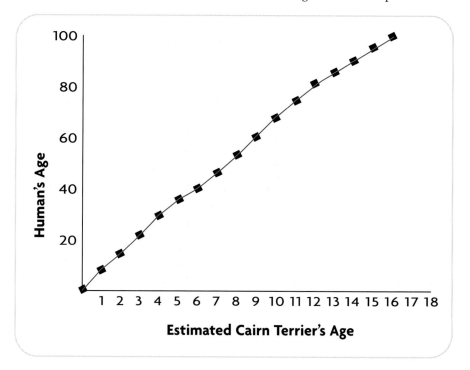

made even more difficult, for not all humans age at the same rate...and human females live longer than human males.

WHAT TO LOOK FOR IN SENIORS

Most veterinarians and behaviorists use the seven-year mark as the time to consider a dog a senior. The term "senior" does not imply that the dog is geriatric and has begun to fail in mind and body. Aging is essentially a slowing process. Humans readily admit that they feel a difference in their activity level from age 20 to 30, and then from 30 to 40, etc. By treating the seven-year-old dog as a senior, owners are able to implement certain therapeutic and preventative medical strategies with the help of their veterinarians. A senior-care

program should include at least two veterinary visits per year, screening sessions to determine the dog's health status, as well as nutritional counseling. Veterinarians determine the senior dog's health status through a blood smear for a complete blood count, serum chemistry profile with electrolytes, urinalysis, blood pressure check, electrocardiogram, ocular tonometry (pressure on the eyeball) and dental prophylaxis.

Such an extensive program for senior dogs is well advised before owners start to see the obvious physical signs of aging, such as slower and inhibited movement, graying, increased

A senior male showing his age on his muzzle. Seniors need special attention from their adoring owners. It's time to show your Cairn how important he is to you and your family.

GETTING OLD

The bottom line is simply that your dog is getting old when you think he is getting old because he slows down in his level of general activity, including walking, running, eating, jumping and retrieving. On the other hand, the frequency of certain activities increases, such as more sleeping, more barking and more repetition of habits like going to the door without being called when you put your coat on to leave the house.

sleep/nap periods and disinterest in play and other activity. This preventative program promises a longer, healthier life for the aging dog. Among the physical problems common in aging dogs are the loss of sight and hearing, arthritis, kidney and liver failure, diabetes mellitus, heart disease and Cushing's disease (a hormonal disease).

In addition to the physical manifestations discussed, there are some behavioral changes and problems related to aging dogs. Dogs suffering from hearing or vision loss, dental discomfort or arthritis can become aggressive. Likewise the near-deaf and/or blind dog may be startled more easily and react in an unexpectedly aggressive manner. Seniors suffering from senility can become more impatient and irritable. Housesoiling accidents are associated with loss of mobility, kidney problems, loss of sphincter control as well as plaque accumulation, physiological brain changes and reactions to medications. Older dogs, just like young puppies, suffer from separation anxiety, which can lead to excessive barking, whining, housesoiling and destructive behavior. Seniors may become fearful of everyday sounds, such as vacuum cleaners, heaters, thunder and passing traffic. Some dogs have difficulty sleeping, due to discomfort, the need for frequent potty visits and the like.

Owners should avoid spoiling the older dog with fatty treats. Obesity is a common problem in older dogs and subtracts years from their lives. Keep the senior dog as trim as possible since excessive weight puts additional stress on the body's vital organs. Some breeders recommend supplementing the diet with foods high in fiber and lower in

NOTICING THE SYMPTOMS

The symptoms listed below are symptoms that gradually appear and become more noticeable. They are not life-threatening; however, the symptoms below are to be taken very seriously and warrant a discussion with your veterinarian:

- Your dog cries and whimpers when he moves, and he stops running completely.
- Convulsions start or become more serious and frequent. The usual convulsion (spasm) is when the dog stiffens and starts to tremble, being unable or unwilling to move. The seizure usually lasts for 5 to 30 minutes.
- Your dog drinks more water and urinates more frequently. Wetting and bowel accidents take place indoors without warning.
- Vomiting becomes more and more frequent.

> **EUTHANASIA**
> Euthanasia must be performed by a licensed veterinarian. There also may be societies for the prevention of cruelty to animals in your area. They often offer this service upon a vet's recommendation.

calories. Adding fresh vegetables and marrow broth to the senior's diet makes a tasty, low-calorie, low-fat supplement. Vets also offer specialty diets for senior dogs that are worth exploring.

Your dog, as he nears his twilight years, needs his owner's patience and good care more than ever. Never punish an older dog for an accident or abnormal behavior. For all the years of love, protection and companionship that your dog has provided, he deserves special attention and courtesies. The older dog may need to relieve himself at 3 a.m. because he can no longer hold it for eight hours. Older dogs may not be able to remain crated for more than two or three hours. It may be time to give up a sofa or chair to your old friend. Although he may not seem as enthusiastic about your attention and petting, he does appreciate the considerations you offer as he gets older.

Your Cairn Terrier does not understand why his world is slowing down. Owners must make the transition into the golden years as pleasant and rewarding as possible.

WHAT TO DO
WHEN THE TIME COMES

You are never fully prepared to make a rational decision about putting your dog to sleep. It is very obvious that you love your Cairn Terrier or you would not be reading this book. Putting a loved dog to sleep is extremely difficult. It is a decision that must be made with your veterinarian. You are usually forced to make the decision when one of the life-threatening symptoms listed above becomes serious enough for you to seek veterinary help.

If the prognosis of the malady indicates the end is near and your beloved pet will only suffer more and experience no enjoyment for the balance of his life, then euthanasia is the right choice.

WHAT IS EUTHANASIA?

Euthanasia derives from the Greek, meaning *good death*. In other words, it means the planned, painless killing of a dog suffering from a painful, incurable condition, or who is so aged that he cannot walk, see, eat or control his excretory functions.

Euthanasia is usually accomplished by injection with an overdose of an anesthesia or

Most pet cemeteries have a suitable resting place for your dog's ashes.

barbiturate. Aside from the prick of the needle, the experience is usually painless.

HOW ABOUT YOU?

The decision to euthanize your dog is never easy. The days during which the dog becomes ill and the end occurs can be unusually stressful for you. If this is your first experience with the death of a loved one, you may need the comfort dictated by your religious beliefs. If you are the head of the family and have children, you should have involved them in the decision of putting your Cairn Terrier to sleep. Usually your dog can be maintained on drugs for a few days in order to give you ample time to make a decision. During this time, talking with members of your family or even people who have lived through this same experience can ease the burden of your inevitable decision.

THE FINAL RESTING PLACE

Dogs can have some of the same privileges as humans. They can occasionally be buried in their entirety in a pet cemetery which is generally expensive, or if they have died at home can be buried in your yard in a place suitably marked with some stone or newly planted tree or bush. Alternatively they can be cremated and the ashes returned to you, or some people prefer to leave their dogs at the vet's office for the vet to dispose of.

All of these options should be discussed frankly and openly with your veterinarian. Do not be afraid to ask financial questions. Cremations can be individual, but a less expensive option is mass cremation, although of course the ashes cannot then be returned. Vets can usually arrange cremation services on your behalf.

GETTING ANOTHER DOG?

The grief of losing your beloved dog will be as lasting as the grief of losing a human friend or relative. In most cases, if your dog died of old age (if there is such a thing), he had slowed down considerably. Do you want a new Cairn Terrier puppy to replace him? Or are you better off in finding a more mature Cairn Terrier,

Views at a typical cemetery for pets. Many cemeteries have a perpetual care plan.

say two to three years of age, which will usually be house-trained and will have an already developed personality. In this case, you can find out if you like each other after a few hours of being together.

The decision is, of course, your own. Do you want another Cairn Terrier or perhaps a different breed so as to avoid comparison with your beloved friend? Most people usually choose the same breed because they know and love the characteristics of that breed. Then, too, they often know people who have the same breed and perhaps they are lucky enough that one of their friends expects a litter soon. What could be better?

SHOWING YOUR
CAIRN TERRIER

When you purchase your Cairn Terrier, you will make it clear to the breeder whether you want one just as a lovable companion and pet, or if you hope to be buying a Cairn Terrier with show prospects. No reputable breeder will sell you a young puppy and tell you that it is *definitely* of show quality, for so

MEET THE AKC

American Kennel Club is the main governing body of the dog sport in the United States. Founded in 1884, the AKC consists of 500 or more independent dog clubs plus 4,500 affiliate clubs, all of which follow the AKC rules and regulations. Additionally, the AKC maintains a registry for pure-bred dogs in the US and works to preserve the integrity of the sport and its continuation in the country. Over 1,000,000 dogs are registered each year, representing about 150 recognized breeds. There are over 15,000 competitive events held annually for which over 2,000,000 dogs enter to participate. Dogs compete to earn over 40 different titles, from Champion to Companion Dog to Master Agility Champion.

much can go wrong during the early months of a puppy's development. If you plan to show, what you will hopefully have acquired is a puppy with "show potential."

To the novice, exhibiting a Cairn Terrier in the show ring may look easy, but it takes a lot of hard work and devotion to do top winning at a show such as the prestigious Westminster Kennel Club dog show, not to mention a little luck too!

The first concept that the canine novice learns when watching a dog show is that each dog first competes against members of its own breed. Once the judge has selected the best member of each breed (Best of Breed), that chosen dog will compete with other dogs in its group. Finally, the dogs chosen first in each group will compete for Best in Show.

The second concept that you must understand is that the dogs are not actually compared against one another. The judge compares each dog against its breed standard, the written description of the ideal specimen that is approved by the American Kennel Club (AKC). While some early breed standards were indeed based on specific dogs

Dog shows can be an exciting and rewarding activity for you and your handsome Cairn.

that were famous or popular, many dedicated enthusiasts say that a perfect specimen, as described in the standard, has never walked into a show ring, has never been bred and, to the woe of dog breeders around the globe, does not exist. Breeders attempt to get as close to this ideal as possible with every litter, but theoretically the "perfect" dog is so elusive that it is impossible. (And if the "perfect" dog were born, breeders and judges probably would never agree that it was indeed "perfect.")

If you are interested in exploring the world of dog showing, your best bet is to join your local breed club or the national (or parent) club, which is the Cairn Terrier Club of America. These clubs often host both regional and national specialties,

shows only for Cairn Terriers, which can include conformation as well as obedience, agility and earthdog events. Even if you have no intention of competing with your Cairn Terrier, a specialty is like a festival for lovers of the breed who congregate to share their favorite topic: Cairn Terriers! Clubs also send out newsletters, and some organize training days and seminars in order that people may learn more about their chosen breed. To locate the breed club closest to you, contact the American Kennel Club, which furnishes the rules and regulations for all of these events plus general dog registration and other basic requirements of dog ownership.

The American Kennel Club offers three kinds of conformation shows: an all-breed show (for all

The world's oldest dog show is the Westminster Kennel Club Dog Show, which takes place annually in New York City. The group finals are completely televised, and the show has an attendance of more than 50,000 people per day.

AKC-recognized breeds), a specialty show (for one breed only, usually sponsored by the parent club) and a group show (for all breeds in the group). For terriers, the most famous group show is the Montgomery County Kennel Club show, held in Pennsylvania every October.

For a dog to become an AKC champion of record, the dog must accumulate 15 points at shows from at least three different judges, including two "majors." A "major" is defined as a three-, four- or five-point win, and the number of points per win is determined on the number of dogs entered in the show on that day. Depending on the breed, the number of points that are awarded varies. At any dog show, only one dog and one bitch of each breed can win points.

Dog showing does not offer "co-ed" classes. Dogs and bitches never compete against each other in the classes. Non-champions are called "class dogs" because they compete in one of five classes. Dogs are entered in particular classes depending on their age and previous show wins. To begin, there is the Puppy Class (for 6- to 9-month-olds and for 9- to 12-month-olds); this class is followed by the Novice Class (for dogs that have not won any first prizes except in the Puppy Class or three first prizes in the Novice Class and have not accumulated any points toward their champion title); the Bred-by-Exhibitor Class (for dogs handled by their breeders or

THE IDEAL DOG

The American Kennel Club defines a standard as: "A description of the ideal dog of each recognized breed, to serve as an ideal against which dogs are judged at shows." This "blueprint" is drawn up by the breed's recognized parent club, approved by a majority of its membership, and then submitted to the AKC for approval. This is a complete departure from the way standards are handled in England, where all standards and changes are controlled by The Kennel Club. The AKC states that "An understanding of any breed must begin with its standard. This applies to all dogs, not just those intended for showing." The picture that the standard draws of the dog's type, gait, temperament and structure is the guiding image used by breeders as they plan their programs.

handled by one of the breeder's immediate family); the American-bred Class (for dogs bred in the US); and the Open Class (for any dog that is not a champion).

The judge at the show begins by judging the Puppy Class, first dogs and then bitches, and proceeds through the classes. The judge places his winners first through fourth in each class. In the Winners Class, the first-place winners of each class compete with one another to determine Winners Dog and Winners Bitch. The judge also places a Reserve Winners Dog and Reserve Winners Bitch, which could be awarded the points in the case of a disqualification. The Winners Dog and Winners Bitch, the two that are awarded the points for the breed, then compete with any champions of record entered in the show. The judge reviews the Winners Dog, Winners Bitch and all of the champions to select his Best of Breed. The Best of Winners is selected between the Winners Dog and Winners Bitch. Were one of these two to be selected Best of Breed, it would automatically be named Best of Winners as well. Finally the judge selects his Best of Opposite Sex to the Best of Breed winner.

At a group show or all-breed show, the Best of Breed winners from each breed then compete against one another in their respective groups for Group One through Group Four. The judge compares each Best of Breed to its breed standard, and the dog that most closely lives up to the ideal for its breed is selected as Group One. Finally, all seven group winners

Preparing for the show can require hours of hard work. Notice the grooming tables. Each dog owner or handler must bring his own grooming tables and supplies.

(from the Terrier Group, Sporting Group, Toy Group, etc.) compete for Best in Show.

To find out about dog shows in your area, you can subscribe to the American Kennel Club's monthly magazine, the *American Kennel Gazette* and the accompanying *Events Calendar.* You can also look in your local newspaper for advertisements for dog shows in your area or go on the Internet to the AKC's website, www.akc.org.

If your Cairn Terrier is six months of age or older and registered with the AKC, you can enter him in a dog show where the breed is offered classes.

Provided that your Cairn Terrier does not have a disqualifying fault, he can compete. Only unaltered dogs can be entered in a dog show, so if you have spayed or neutered your Cairn Terrier, he cannot compete in conformation shows. The reason for this is simple. Dog shows are the main forum to prove which representatives in a breed are worthy of being bred. Only dogs that have achieved championships—the AKC "seal of approval" for quality in pure-bred dogs—should be bred. Altered dogs, however, can participate in other AKC events such as obedience trials and the

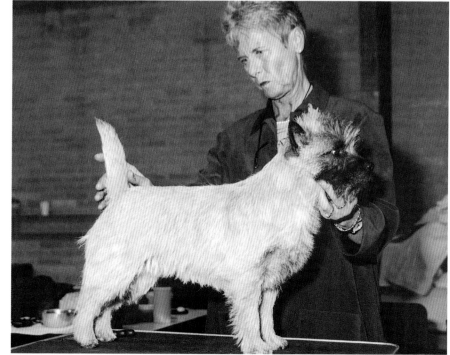

This young Cairn is being exhibited for the first time in the ring. It is unusual that a young dog will do well beyond the Puppy Class, so don't be disheartened if you are not selected at your very first show.

The handler must be attentive to the judge's wishes during the physical examination. Your Cairn must be trained to tolerate the handling of a stranger in order to compete in a dog show.

Canine Good Citizen® program.

Before you actually step into the ring, you would be well advised to sit back and observe the judge's ring procedure. If it is your first time in the ring, do not be over-anxious and run to the front of the line. It is much better to stand back and study how the exhibitor in front of you is performing. The judge asks each handler to stand, or "stack," the dog, hopefully showing the dog off to his best advantage. The judge will observe the dog from a distance and from different angles, and approach the dog to check his teeth, overall structure, alertness and muscle tone, descended testicles in males, as well as consider how well the dog

CLUB CONTACTS

You can get information about dog shows from the national kennel clubs:

American Kennel Club
5580 Centerview Dr., Raleigh, NC 27606-3390
www.akc.org

United Kennel Club
100 E. Kilgore Road, Kalamazoo, MI 49002
www.ukcdogs.com

Canadian Kennel Club
89 Skyway Ave., Suite 100, Etobicoke, Ontario
M9W 6R4 Canada
www.ckc.ca

The Kennel Club
1-5 Clarges St., Piccadilly
London W1Y 8AB, UK
www.the-kennel-club.org.uk

"conforms" to the standard. Most importantly, the judge will have the exhibitor move the dog around the ring in some pattern that he should specify (another advantage to not going first, but always listen since some judges change their directions—and the judge is always right!). Finally, the judge will give the dog one last look before moving on to the next exhibitor.

If you are not in the top four in your class at your first show, do not be discouraged. Be patient and consistent, and you may eventually find yourself in a winning line-up. Remember that the winners were once in your shoes and have devoted many hours and much

money to earn the placement. If you find that your dog is losing every time and never getting a nod, it may be time to consider a different dog sport or to just enjoy your Cairn Terrier as a pet. Parent clubs offer other events, such as agility, tracking, obedience, earthdog and instinct tests which may be of interest to the owner of a well-trained Cairn Terrier.

EARTHDOG TESTS
Interest in promoting the natural ability of Cairn Terriers has exploded in the US, and earthdog tests, sponsored by the American Kennel Club, have become an exciting part of Cairn Terrier

This is what its all about...winning! This dog took Best of Breed and Group One, proving that he was the best Terrier entered that day.

ownership. These tests are enjoyed by the show-dog set as well as by everyday pet owners. According to AKC rules, Cairn Terriers must be six months of age to participate in the tests and can compete at four class levels, including Introduction to Quarry, Junior Earthdog, Senior Earthdog and Master Earthdog. Artificial or live quarry is used in these tests, though cages protect the rats from physical (if not psychological) harm. The stated purpose of earthdog tests is to provide the dogs the chance to demonstrate their natural talent in following and pursuing game.

OBEDIENCE TRIALS

Obedience trials in the US trace back to the early 1930s, when organized obedience training was developed to demonstrate how well dog and owner could work together. The pioneer of obedience trials is Mrs. Helen Whitehouse Walker, a Standard Poodle fancier, who designed a series of exercises after the Associated Sheep, Police Army Dog Society of Great Britain. Since the days of Mrs. Walker, obedience trials have grown by leaps and bounds, and today there are over 2,000 trials held in the US every year, with more than 100,000 dogs competing. Any registered AKC or ILP (Indefinite Listing Privilege) dog can enter an obedience trial, regardless of conformational disqualifications or neutering.

CANINE GOOD CITIZEN® PROGRAM

Have you ever considered getting your dog "certified"? The AKC's Canine Good Citizen® program affords your dog just that opportunity. Your dog is a well-behaved canine citizen, using the basic training and good manners you have taught him, takes a series of ten tests that illustrate that he can behave properly at home, in a public place and around other dogs. The tests are administered by participating dog clubs, colleges, 4-H clubs, scouts and other community groups and are open to all pure-bred and mixed-breed dogs. Upon passing the ten tests, the suffix CGC is then applied to your dog's name.

The ten tests are: 1. Accepting a friendly stranger; 2. Sitting politely for petting; 3. Appearance and grooming; 4. Walking on a lead; 5. Walking through a group of people; 6. Sit, down and stay on command; 7. Coming when called; 8. Meeting another dog; 9. Calm reaction to distractions; 10. Separation from owner.

Obedience trials are divided into three levels of progressive difficulty. At the first level, the Novice, dogs compete for the title Companion Dog (CD); at the intermediate level, the Open, dogs compete for the title Companion Dog Excellent (CDX); and at the advanced level, the

Utility, dogs compete for the title Utility Dog (UD). Classes are subdivided into "A" (for beginners) and "B" (for more experienced handlers). A perfect score at any level is 200, and a dog must score 170 or better to earn a "leg," of which three are needed to earn the title. To earn points, the dog must score more than 50% of the available points in each exercise; the possible points range from 20 to 40.

Once a dog has earned the UD title, he can compete with other proven obedience dogs for the coveted title of Utility Dog Excellent (UDX), which requires that the dog win "legs" in ten shows. In 1977, the title Obedience Trial Champion (OTCh.) was established by the AKC. Utility Dogs who earn "legs" in Open B and Utility B earn points toward their Obedience Trial Champion title. To become an OTCh., a dog needs to earn 100 points, which requires three first places in Open B and Utility under three different judges.

The Grand Prix of obedience trials, the AKC National Obedience Invitational, gives qualifying Utility Dogs the chance to win the newest and highest title: National Obedience Champion (NOC). Only the top 25 ranked obedience dogs, plus any dog ranked in the top 3 in its breed, are allowed to compete.

TRACKING

Any dog is capable of tracking, using his nose to follow a trail. The Cairn Terrier has done quite well in tracking tests, just as he has done in obedience trials, though not as well as breeds like the Bloodhound or Border Collie. The AKC started tracking tests in 1937, when the first licensed test took place as part of the Utility level at an obedience trial. Ten years later, in 1947, the AKC offered the first title, Tracking Dog (TD). It was not until 1980 that the AKC added the Tracking Dog Excellent title (TDX), which was followed by the Versatile Surface Tracking title (VST) in 1995. The title Champion Tracker (CT) is awarded to a dog who has earned all three titles.

AGILITY TRIALS

Having had its origins in the UK back in 1977, agility had its official AKC beginning in August 1994, when the first licensed agility trials were held. The AKC allows all registered breeds (including Miscellaneous Class breeds) to participate, providing the dog is 12 months of age or older. Agility is designed so that the handler demonstrates how well the dog can work at his side. The handler directs his dog over an obstacle course that includes jumps as well as tires, the dog walk, weave poles, pipe tunnels, collapsed tunnels, etc. While working his way through the course, the dog must keep one eye and ear on the handler and the rest of his body on the course. The handler gives verbal and hand signals to guide the dog through the course.

The first organization to promote agility trials in the US was the United States Dog Agility Association, Inc. (USDAA), which was established in 1986 and spawned numerous member clubs around the country. Both the USDAA and the AKC offer titles to winning dogs. Three titles are available through the USDAA: Agility Dog (AD), Advanced Agility Dog (AAD) and Master Agility Dog (MAD). The AKC offers Novice Agility (NA), Open Agility (OA), Agility Excellent (AX) and Master Agility Excellent (MX). Beyond these four AKC titles, dogs can win additional ones in "jumper" classes, Jumpers with Weave Novice (NAJ), Open (OAJ) and Excellent (MXJ), which lead to the ultimate title(s): MACH, Master Agility Champion. Dogs can continue to add number designations to the MACH titles, indicating how many times the dog has met the MACH requirements, such as MACH1, MACH2, etc.

Agility is great fun for dog and owner, with many rewards for everyone involved. Interested owners should join a training club that has obstacles and experienced agility handlers who can introduce you and your dog to the "ropes" (and tires, tunnels, etc.).

The Cairn Terrier won second in the Group at England's famous Crufts Show in 1999. Winning the Group was a Norwich Terrier.

INDEX

*Page numbers in **boldface** indicate illustrations.*

My Cairn Terrier

PUT YOUR PUPPY'S FIRST PICTURE HERE

Dog's Name _____

Date _____ Photographer _____